YOUR FIRST JOB

The Recent Grad's Indispensable Guide to Getting a Job!

Dan Quillen

Author of *The Perfect Resume, The Perfect Interview,* and *Get a Job! How I Found a Job When Jobs are Hard to Find – And So Can You!*

Cold Spring Press

Get a Job! series

Your First Job is the fourth in the **Get a Job! series** of books written by Dan Quillen. Once again, Quillen calls on his expertise as an HR professional (and as one who lost and found a job in the toughest economic environment since the Great Depression) to help recent grads understand the New Economy, and how to find work when many cannot.

CITATIONS

Sophia Amoruso quote: www.brainyquote.com/quotes/quotes/s/sophiaamor703853.html

Robert Anthony quote: www.brainyquote.com/quotes/quotes/r/robertanth125911.html?src=t_graduation

Arthur Ashe quote: www.brainyquote.com/quotes/quotes/a/arthurashe109755.html

Drew Barrymore quote: www.brainyquote.com/quotes/quotes/d/drewbarrym129676.html?src=t_in_the_end

Wade Boggs quote: www.brainyquote.com/quotes/quotes/w/wadeboggs311616.html?src=t_positive_attitude

Marcus Buckingham Quote: www.brainyquote.com/quotes/quotes/m/marcusbuck526900.html

Chanakya quote: www.brainyquote.com/quotes/quotes/c/chanakya201078.html#4lX6wsac69EXME50.99

Anthony D'Angelo quote: www.brainyquote.com/quotes/quotes/a/anthonyjd384468.html

Mike Davidson quote: www.brainyquote.com/quotes/quotes/m/mikedavids230205.html

Albert Einstein quote: www.brainyquote.com/quotes/quotes/a/alberteins109012.html

Helen Hayes quote: http://sayquotable.com/the-expert-in-anything-was-once-a-beginner

A. P. J. Abdul Kalam quote: www.brainyquote.com/quotes/quotes/a/apjabdu384108.html

Chelsea Krost quote: http://launchingcreative.com]

Edward Norton quote: www.brainyquote.com/quotes/quotes/e/edwardnort449658.html

Hannibal Smith quote: www.thisdayinquotes.com/2011/01/i-love-it-when-plan-comes-together.html

Will Smith quote: www.brainyquote.com/quotes/keywords/good_job.html#Om7Pr2ST59WfjSi8.99

Mark Twain quotes: www.brainyquote.com/search_results.html?q=clothes+make+the+man www.brainyquote.com/quotes/quotes/m/marktwain103892.html

PRAISE FOR DAN'S JOB-SEARCH BOOKS!

"I was out of work for almost 2 years, and was just not getting many responses from the resumes I was sending out. I picked up a copy of Dan's book and began following his counsel in a number of areas, especially related to resumes and interviewing. Within 3 weeks, I had 4 interviews and received two job offers. I am now happily employed with a great job and feel like following Dan's counsel is the primary reason I was able to get these job offers and land my job." – *Jeremy Savage*

"Dan Quillen knows what he is talking about in this book. I took his advice and had a job within 3 weeks of being laid off. Buy it today and it will set you on a direct course to success!" – *Lynette W. Fox*

"Mr. Quillen's book is an easy read with a great deal of helpful information. Having been a hiring manager and HR director, as well as having been laid off himself during the recent recession, Mr. Quillen has a particular expertise that others may not. This book is also written with a focus on how techniques in job searching have changed in recent years, due to technology and the economy. I highly recommend this book to those that are either newly unemployed or wishing to make a change." – *Debra S. Heglin*

"If you want to spend your money wisely on creating a résumé that will result in interviews and therefore job offers, this book will take you further and more expeditiously than most so-called experts. He gives clear, simple, succinct direction in *Get a Job!* to create a résumé that will get the interview to get the job! Don't skip any chapters!" – *Ginny Ford, Ford Personnel, Inc.*

"I have been recommending *The Perfect Resume* to all my candidates. I love the content and the order of things that are presented in Dan's book." – *Sally S. Cohen, President, The Arundel Group*

COLD SPRING PRESS

www.get-a-great-job.com

Copyright © 2015 by W. Daniel Quillen
ISBN 13: 978-1-59360-214-7
Library of Congress Control Number: 2015947850

ABOUT THE AUTHOR

Dan Quillen is the author of *Get a Job! – How I Found a Job When Jobs are Hard to Find, And So Can You!, The Perfect Resume* and *The Perfect Interview*. He has been a professional in Human Resources for 25 years. For a decade, he was the Director of Human Resources for one of the largest law firms in the western United States. Currently he is the Director of Internal Services (managing Human Resources, Purchasing, Risk and Fleet) for the City of Aurora, the third largest city in Colorado.

Dan has long been an active mentor for those who are out of work, freely sharing his expertise in résumé review and creation, interviewing and job searching. A few years ago Dan was laid off and had the opportunity to try the techniques he has been teaching others for years. In Dan's books, he shares the knowledge and techniques that allowed him to find a job in a short period of time during the worst economic downturn our country has had since the Great Depression.

When not doing HR, Dan is a professional writer specializing in travel, technical, genealogy, and how-to subjects. He has written and published 15 books on various topics. Dan makes his home in Centennial, Colorado. If you'd like to contact Dan about anything in this book, his e-mail address is: wdanielquillen@gmail.com, and he welcomes your comments and questions.

Table of Contents

Introduction

Thank you for buying *Your First Job: The Recent Grad's Indispensable Guide to Getting a Job*. If you've purchased this book, or it has been given to you by a friend or family member (probably your mother!), it probably means your four+ (6+, 8+...) years of formal schooling have come to an end, or will soon be coming to an end, and it's time to find job to which you can apply all that "book learning."

Alas, that may also mean you have been greeted rather rudely by the **New Economy**. The New Economy began in the 2007 / 2008 timeframe, and we are still suffering from its symptoms: high unemployment rates, even higher underemployment rates, hundreds of candidates for each good job.

While the economy is slowly improving – it is still nothing to shout about (scream and holler, perhaps). The government continues to feed us a line about the improving economy, but looking closely tells us that the economy is still fragile – jobs being created are not typically career jobs – they are 25- to 29-hour per week jobs (below the hours minimum for benefits such as health insurance due to Obamacare requirements). And the news in the New Economy is particularly tough on recent college graduates. The latest Department of Labor statistics tell us that new grads with Bachlors' degrees could expect sobering and staggering employment news – 8.5% unemployment and 16.8% underemployment – characterized by those who have accepted employment as baristas and bike messengers to landscapers and administrative assistants rather than in the fields of work for which they studied (and paid big buck$ to earn that degree). Nearly half (44%) of college grads won't find work that requires the degree they earned, and the salaries that 50% will earn will be between $25,000 and $45,000 – making it tough to pay back those mounds of student loans many recent college grads carry with them.

When you hear that unemployment numbers have dropped yet again, be aware that the numbers do not include anyone that has been unemployed for longer than about three and a half months, nor anyone who has taken part-time work because nothing else was available. Economic researchers smarter than I am estimate the actual unemployment rate is triple what is reported (some feel it's about five to six times higher than the official unemployment number). I tell you this so that you don't unnecessarily beat yourself up – how could you not find employment when the unemployment rate is so low!? Well, now you know – the unemployment rate is not as low as some would have us believe.

Unemployment numbers are signficantly under-reported

The New Economy we find ourselves in today means that more young people – recent graduates -- are unemployed or underemployed than at any time since the Great Depression – eight decades ago! It means that nearly every job for which graduates compete has scores, if not hundreds, of applicants. It also means that hiring managers and Human Resource departments are understaffed compared to just a few years ago, so they have turned to applications software to screen the majority of resumes and applications down to a manageable number that can be reviewed personally.

Through the pages of this book we'll speak about topics that should help you in your job search. You've worked hard the last four+ years to get to this point in your life. Now there are things you can do to help increase your chances of landing a job that will help you earn your way in this New Economy. We'll discuss things like resumes and preparing for interviews, networking and persistence, planning and following through on your job search, and what to do once you get that job you've worked so hard to earn.

Not a college graduate?

Are you still a student – haven't yet graduated from college? All the better! There are things you can do now that will help pave the way for when you do graduate, and if you are diligent you may be able to slip right from the graduation podium to the workplace.

INTRODUCTION

You haven't yet gone to college? You're just graduating from high school and wonder what you should do? Can't decide whether you should work for a while before going to college? Or – should you go to college at all? Good – I have a chapter specifically designed for you later on in this book. But don't just skip over all the chapters between here and there – many of the concepts I discuss in between have as much application to you as they do to someone who has completed their college education – resume advice, interview preparation and counseling, planning your job search, etc.

In recent years, the place where I work has historically had many candidates for each job. The last few years, we have seen the volume of candidates drop, but the quality of candidates has remained high – BAs and MBAs are looking for work in record numbers. Still, even with the numbers of candidates dwindling, you must still be on your "A" game to get an interview and earn a job. It is not uncommon at all for us to have over 100 applicants for jobs, and sometimes as many as 300 applicants. Through the pages of this book, I will share how best to beat the numbers game and have your resume considered, as well as to receive an interview, and then how to prepare for and then perform during the interview so that you are the selected candidate.

What qualifies *this* guy to write *this* book?

I have been a Human Resource professional for over two decades, and for longer than that, I have been a hiring manager. I know what hiring managers and HR departments look for when screening applicants for

> **The competition is tough ... but I can do it!**

positions. And – perhaps more important – I know what works and what does not work for applicants when it comes to finding work.

Does this guy know anything about finding work in the New Economy?

Absolutely. Several years ago, at the height of the Recession, I found myself suddenly out of work. I walked the path you are walking, and I know what it takes to get in front of hiring managers, and what it takes to earn an interview. I have done it, and I have done it in the New Economy. During my short time as an unemployed worker, I applied for 130 positions. I was successful in getting 31 interviews – nearly a one-in-four hit rate. I succeeded in getting that ratio of interviews when my peers were getting one interview for every 20 or 25 resumes they submitted. Through the pages of this book, I will share how you can also have that kind of success.

Does this guy know anything about helping young graduates find work in the New Economy?

Yes! I have had and continue to have significant experience assisting young people – college grads, college students and high school graduates – find work in this economy. I have worked with recent college grads as they have sought employment, and have cheered their successes. Whether one of my own six children, recent graduates from my church and children of friends, college grads that are referred to me by friends and work associates, I have critical insights into what it's like to search for work as a recent graduate in this economy. And we've had more than a few successes in finding work for them!

Why is this guy writing this book?

I have to be honest (I always am!) – it appalls me to see how little so many candidates know about searching for jobs. It is almost stunning to see the naiveté of many job searchers on an almost daily basis. That was one of the reasons I wrote *Get a Job!* – the first in this series of books about finding a job in the New Economy, and why I have now written this book for recent graduates and current college students.

My hope is that through the pages of this book you can learn key principles to successfully plan and execute your job search. The operative word in that last sentence is *successfully* – even though I do not know you personally, one of my goals is to assist you in finding meaningful work.

I am interested in hearing how things are going in your job search. When you have a chance, please e-mail me at wdanielquillen@gmail.com and let me know how it is going, your successes and even your questions.

Overview

In the **Introduction**, you learned a bit about the New Economy – the economy within which you are seeking employment. You learned that the unemployment number reported publically by the government bears little resemblance to the truth, and that unemployment is much higher… and that is true for those who are recent college graduates.

In this chapter, I'll give you a quick preview of the things you'll find in the ensuing chapters.

In **The Millennials** chapter, you'll learn more about Millennials and the role they'll (you'll!) play in the workforce of the near future. You'll learn about stereotypes that are held about Millennials – both flattering and not so flattering. Understanding these stereotypes is important to learning how to deal with them.

In the **Things To Do Before You Graduate** chapter, you'll learn the importance of paying attention to your grades (sorry to have to mention that!), tips for interviewing for internships and job interviews with on-campus recruiters, etc. We also discuss the importance of determining what you want to be when you grow up.

In the **Plan Your Work, Work Your Plan** chapter, I share how important it is to organize your job search and stick to your plan. Having a plan will help you reach your goals – including that of becoming employed.

In the **Stay Positive** chapter, my counsel is to do just that – stay positive. There is no question this may be a difficult time in your life, but staying positive will help you weather this time, and may well be the difference between finding a job quickly and having to wait awhile. If you are negative, you may think, "Ah, what's the use?" and you back off your job hunt for a few weeks (or months). But – what if the perfect job for you was posted during your pouting time, and you didn't apply for it? You'll never know, of course, but let that thought work in the back of your mind to spur you on to consistent job search efforts. I even provide ten keys to making it through your time of unemployment.

In the **Your Resume / Some Experience** chapter, I address this critical element in your job hunt arsenal. I share my thoughts as a hiring manager, someone who has looked at tens of thousands of resumes throughout my career. I have some strong opinions about resumes, and I share those throughout the chapter. Perhaps the most important lesson from that chapter is that one-size-doesn't-fit-all when it comes to resumes. In today's job search market, each resume you submit must be tailored specifically to the requirements of the job for which you are applying. I share excerpts from several resumes to demonstrate my thoughts on each section. I share my thoughts on the importance of effectively proofreading your resume, and I list a few common typos I run across when reviewing resumes (sad to say!).

In **Your Resume / No Experience** chapter, building on the previous resume chapter, I show you how to improve your resume and your job search overall even if you have no work experience.

In the **Cover Letters** chapter, I address how important cover letters are when applying for a job. I know some hiring managers who don't even look at cover letters, but I also know hiring managers who look at cover letters, and if they are interested further in the candidate, they'll look at their resume. Why take a chance on not providing a cover letter?

In the **Network, Network, Network!** chapter, I speak about the importance of networking to find a position. It is such an important tool that it deserves its own chapter. I'll also provide tips on how to get started, who and what your networks are, etc.

In the **Social Networking** chapter, I discuss the value of using social media like LinkedIn, Facebook and Twitter to expand your network and help you find jobs.

In the **Best Job Search Sites for Recent Grads** chapter, I provide a listing and description of the top job search websites for college students.

In the **Before the Interview** chapter, I address how to prepare for that interview you've finally been able to get. It includes learning all you can about the company with which you will be interviewing, using your networks to learn more about the company or the hiring manager (and perhaps to even have a good word provided to the hiring manager before the interview), and selecting an "interview suit." The chapter will finish with a section about preparing ahead of time for questions that might be asked during the interview. I discuss how best to sell yourself, how to handle dangerous questions, and how to prepare for and answer those questions you hope never get asked.

In **The Interview** chapter, I go over how to thrive during the interview you have worked so hard to get. I introduce the 20-20-20 concept: the first twenty feet, first twenty seconds and first twenty words – the only time you will have to make a first impression on your hiring manager. I review things like dressing for success, arriving on time, and learning and using the interviewers' names during the interview. I talk about the fact that, counter-intuitively, the interview isn't about you – it's about the company. Hiring managers are looking for someone who can help their company, solve a problem, and fit well into their culture and team. Keep that in mind as you interview: what can you offer the hiring manager that will solve his / her problems?

In the **Gatekeepers** chapter, I share my thoughts on who some of the gatekeepers are – people who have the power to keep you from interviewing with the company or hiring manager – and how to get around them. Gatekeepers included well-meaning secretaries, HR departments and recruiting software packages.

In the **Are You Too Young for this Job?** chapter, I address the possibility that you may face some age discrimination during your job search due to your youthfulness and lack of experience.

In the **Temp Agencies – Yes or No?** chapter, you'll learn about the value temporary agencies can be in your job search. They provide an employment foot in the door, as companies often turn to temp agencies for support, and end up hiring (or not) the employees who come to them through the temp agencies.

In the **For High School Grads** chapter, I provide counsel that is tailored to high school students. Among other things, I stress the importance of continuing your education to position yourself for great opportunities in the future. I explore some of your options, including working before you go off to school, some college, bachelor's or master's degrees, vocational / trade schools and the military.

In my **In Summary** chapter, I close out by refreshing your memory on a few of the critical elements in the job search business you're now in.

The Millennials

I think Millennials are a generation unlike anything we've ever seen on this planet.
-- Chelsea Krost

Many of you reading this book are known as **Millennials** (also known in some circles as Generation Y) – that segment of the US population born between roughly 1980 and the early 2000s. If you're like most Millennials, you resist labels – you are who you are, not a part of some other group. And I can appreciate that. However, despite that, study after study shows that individuals born during that twenty-plus years share many of the same attributes….or, more precisely, they share at least a perception of the same attributes. That is important to you as you begin looking for work.

Whether those stereotypical perceptions are true of you or not, you need to understand they are or may be held by a significant portion of the population – and most relevant to you – they may be held by hiring managers and/or HR professionals. If some of those perceptions about you are wrong, then you need to do something to let the career decision makers in your life know they are wrong. First of all, let's look at a couple of the perceptions that may be out there. A quick trip around the Internet searching for *Millennial stereotypes* yielded the following stereotypes:

• Confident
• Creative
• Connected
• Technologically savvy

• Interested in meaningful work (work that provides more than just a paycheck)
• Open to Change

Now those aren't bad at all; but here are a few others that aren't quite as positive that you may have to battle as you seek opportunities in the work place:

• Narcissistic (egotistical, it's all about me, etc.)
• Lazy
• Living at home
• Painfully / brutally honest
• Tattooed
• Ladened with trophies, often undeserved (participation trophies)
• Can't take constructive criticism
• You want it all now – VP, corner office, etc.

Those aren't quite as flattering as the first six!

I do not share this information to make you feel bad (the last eight entries above) or to swell your head (the first six entries). I share the information with you so you are armed with knowledge. If you interview with someone who holds those perceptions of you as a Millennial – whether good or ill – you need to be aware of that. In the *Are You Too Young for this Job?* chapter in this book, I provide you with tools that will help you deal with those negative perceptions. So until you get to that chapter in this book, just muse on those stereotypes – good and ill.

Notwithstanding those potential negative impressions, there is a lot of good news for Millennials! Economic / demographic researchers estimate that 46% of the US workforce will be Millennials by the year 2020. That's an amazing statistic, and indicates that many Baby Boomers (those born between 1946 and 1964) are retiring. Their positions will be taken by the generation born between 1964 and 1980 (Generation X) and by Millennials – what a great opportunity for you!

But – that can only happen if you can get your foot in the proverbial employment door. In order to move *up* in a company, you have to be *in* the company.

> By 2020, nearly half the workforce will be Millenials and Gen Xers – including me!

And that's where this book comes in – we'll talk about a variety of things you can do to get that door open, and to secure a job in the area which you have studied, the segment of the workforce you wish to be in.

The Millennials checklist

_____ Am I a Millennial (born between 1980 and the early 2000s)?

_____ Be aware of stereotypes that may be held about individuals of my generation.

_____ There are many positive stereotypes of my generation…but there are also some negative ones.

_____ Awareness of stereotypes helps me deal with them more effectively.

_____ 46% of the US workforce is expected to be Millennials and Gen Xers by 2020 – that means there will be many opportunities for me!

4 Things to Do Before You Graduate

Some people drink from the fountain of knowledge, others just gargle.
– Robert Anthony

If your mom (dad, uncle, mentor, best friend, sibling…) gave you this book before you graduate, you're in luck. There are some things you can do now to facilitate gaining a job after you graduate. Here are a few:

What do you want to be when you grow up?
This may sound downright silly, but well before you walk across that stage and accept your diploma from the dean of your school, you need to know what you want to be when you grow up…or at least what you want to be once you graduate.

You need to have a plan – an objective for what you want to do when you graduate. Just because you are a newly minted MBA, BSBA, or another degree, don't expect companies to rush you with job offers. You must decide what you want to do and where you want to do it. Do you want to work in the private sector (for-profit companies)? These are companies that will likely pay higher salaries than non-profit organizations (charities, municipalities, counties, state or federal government, schools, etc.). However, you may feel you want to give back to the community that reared you, and so working in the government sector is where you want to be, even it if means you'll have to take a little less salary.

And of course, it's best if these plans are made well in advance of your graduation. Knowing where you are headed helps you plan the journey more effectively, helps you take classes that will prepare you for your choice of profession. If you know what you want to do early enough, it will help you as you seek an internship that may lead to immediate employment upon graduation.

So many good things can happen to you and your career with just a little forethought and planning. Speak with fellow students, former students – those who graduated a year or two or three before you – to see what they are doing, what they are finding in their work, etc. Learn from them – from their successes as well as the bumps in their career roads.

Haunt your school's Career Center, and listen to what they have to say. They are there to serve the students of your university – take advantage of their expertise and assistance. And – don't wait until the week before you graduate to do this – start early in your college career to see what they have to offer, and stay in touch with them frequently.

Speak with your parents and other older working adults you respect. See what suggestions they may have. Their experience and insights may be invaluable to you as you prepare for your own career.

Grades

Please pay attention to your grades – they often make a significant difference when you are applying for a position. Unless you are attending or are recently graduated from one of the nation's best schools – Harvard, Yale, Princeton, Stanford, etc. – a stellar grade point average and class ranking can make a significant difference in the options available to you, and will open career doors for you (or close them, as the case may be).

I used to be the Director of Human Resources for one of the largest law firms in the western United States – the firm had over 250 attorneys. 40% of our attorneys were from the Top Ten rated law schools (Yale, Harvard, Stanford, Columbia, etc.). For students from those institutions, our Director of Legal Recruiting paid little attention to GPAs or class rank. But if you weren't from one of those top-tier schools, our next preference was students who attended the law schools that were ranked 11 through 50. Generally, to be considered for employment at our firm if you attended one of those schools, you had to be in the top 10% of your class.

Now, I understand that relatively few of us can afford to attend the top ten (or even top fifty) schools in the nation. But that's okay – there are still many opportunities available for those who don't attend those uber-premier schools. Just be aware that an easy way to separate candidates is by GPA. So please, pay attention to your grades.

Grades matter – buckle down!

Many companies will ask for your GPA in your field of study – so they're not interested in those general studies courses you took during your first few years of school and piled up an impressive GPA. They are interested in how well you did in your degree area, whether it is engineering, political science, communications, accounting, human resources, or whatever. So pay attention to your grades in your junior and senior years, as you take those upper division and degree-related classes.

Internships

My strongest counsel to students still in college (next to focusing on your grades) is to actively seek an internship between your junior and senior years, even between your sophomore and junior years as well. These are nothing more than six- or eight-week job interviews, and provide you with that foot in the employment door. So when on-campus interviews are being announced for your campus, be sure you give them the utmost attention. Prior to going to the interviews, research the various companies that will be on campus, and have handy facts you can share about the company, sort of like name dropping, so the recruiters know you went the extra mile to learn something about their company.

In addition to on-campus interviews for internships, companies also visit campuses on recruiting trips – looking for newly graduated students to join their company. The following tips apply to these interviews as well as to interviews for internships.

During one period of my career, I had the opportunity to do on-campus interviews, and I know a number of on-campus recruiters. Here are a few tips to having successful on-campus interviews:

Interview early. Prioritize the companies you'll be interviewing with, and interview as early as possible with those companies. Recruiters get tired by the end of the interviewing day, and as the interview day grinds along, candidates often aren't as sharp either. If you have no other choice but to interview with your favorite company until late in the day, then mentally prepare yourself to be up and energetic.

Be open. Be open to other companies besides the very top companies in your field. Not everyone will get an internship with Google, IBM, Microsoft, etc., and the competition (not to mention the sheer numbers) for these Blue Chip companies will be stiff. But there may be other companies who are on campus that may provide great opportunities for you. Just because they're not Google, don't turn your nose up at them. And – this probably goes without saying (but I'll say it anyway) -- don't let the "other" company sense that you consider them as less impressive or a less desirable place to work than Google, IBM, etc.

Research the company. As mentioned above, research the company, and then let the recruiter know you have done so. It doesn't have to be anything significant; it can be as simple as, "I saw on your website that you were expanding into Mexico. I am fluent in Spanish, and wonder if I might be able to use my language skills to assist in that area of your company." See, you just let them know you did research on their company, and that you are fluent in a foreign language that may be of value to them!

Dress appropriately for the interviews. Yes, recruiters understand you're a poor college student; but you need to dress appropriately for your interviews.

Differentiate yourself as a candidate. By and large, all college students are homogenous – young, eager, excited about the opportunities, little formal experience but a lot of book learning. But is there something about you that will make you stand out as different? If you can differentiate yourself, you may differentiate yourself right into an internship. You are fluent in another language? Tell them! President of your Sorority? Let them know.

Do not be a know-it-all. A pet peeve of mine (and many recruiters and hiring managers, for that matter) are candidates who come across as know-it-alls. These are people who try to prove to you how well they know your industry, market, field of labor, etc. The fact of the matter is unless you've worked in the industry, the secretary you are assigned once you are hired will most likely know more about the industry than you do, and s/he'll know more than you for several years. Sometimes, there is no substitute for experience. And as much as you feel you've learned in your classes, you have just scratched the surface of the knowledge you will have after one, two, three, five, ten years in the industry. So – don't try to blow the recruiters away with your industry knowledge, because you're likely to crash and burn (whether you know it or not!). Recruiters, hiring managers and HR personnel who interview new graduates understand that you don't know everything…in fact, they understand you don't know much of anything, and that most of what you think you know will likely be over-shadowed by the things you'll learn as you begin working for their company. So be cautious that you don't come across as a know-it-all in your interview.

Agressively seek an internship

Networking

Networking is a word that gets thrown around out there a lot as it relates to job searches, and rightfully so. Study after study shows that between 60% and 70% of the jobs obtained in this country are secured through networking. To ignore networking is to ignore perhaps the greatest tool you have at your disposal when it comes to job hunting.

I have worked with many job seekers – recent college grads, unemployed men and women, etc., who relate that the term *networking* strikes fear into their souls, and causes them to break out into a cold sweat.

And it needn't do that.

You can be a very effective networker by simply speaking with the people you know. The people in your church, synagogue, mosque, etc. Roommates, former room-mates, professors, friends on Facebook, tweeple on Twitter and connections on LinkedIn. Get the word out and let them know you are seeking employment.

My son owes his first job as an attorney to a conversation he had with an attorney who graduated a year ahead of him from law school. My son (Michael) knew this young man and reached out to him to see if his firm was hiring, or if he knew any firms in the area who were doing so. The answers were "Yes" and "Yes," and within a short time, Michael had a job offer in hand during what many industry experts agree was the most difficult employment year for law school graduates in many, many years (2009).

As you put the word out among your friends and acquaintances, be sure and be specific – don't make them guess what you're looking for. Tell them when you're graduating, what your degree is in, and the kinds of jobs you're interested in.

Be Flexible
As you begin your job search, there is a direct corollary between how flexible you are and how fast you will find a job. If you gate your job search by city, state or region of the country, you may unnecessarily be setting up roadblocks to your success. You're from a small town in Illinois and you'll only consider work there? The opportunities in your hometown may be limited, and as good as you are, if there are not any jobs available, you'll not get one. The more flexible you can be, the more likely you are to land a job. I once worked with a woman – a recent college grad and single mother, who insisted that she would only work within a small radius from her home, and that she must work only 9:00am to 3:00pm. Those gating factors made it very dif-

ficult to find a job. In fact, it was not until she loosened up her restrictions that she even began receiving interviews.

As we were beginning our marriage and working career, my wife and I decided we would not gate our opportunities. We were westerners (Arizona and Colorado), but we decided we could probably live anywhere for at least a few years. If the place we selected didn't fit our lifestyle for any reason, we figured we could still live there for a few years while I gained experience that allowed me to move to other, more desirable locations. My first career job after school was in Boise, Idaho – a city I had never even visited before the weekend prior to my start date with my new company. We stayed there 18 months, then moved to Salt Lake City, Utah.

After working in Salt Lake City for four years, my boss called me into his office. He asked me if I wanted to be a Technical Consultant for AT&T the rest of my life. I told him no, that I was hoping to progress in the company. He pointed out that for me to progress in the company, the next logical step for me was to be promoted into his job, and he wasn't expecting to be promoted, to retire or to die for many years to come!

He strongly suggested that I consider seeking opportunities within the company in our regional offices in Denver, Colorado, or even better, at our corporate offices in New Jersey. My wife and I discussed it, and once again decided not to put restrictions on our opportunities, and within a short time we were living and working in New Jersey. (For what it's worth – we loved living in New Jersey!)

I worked in our corporate headquarters for four years, and the two jobs I had and the experience I gained while working in New Jersey enabled us to accept another great career opportunity in Colorado – one of the states we had decided we'd like to live in. That experience led to many others and to the career I was able to fashion in several industries. Had I set out on my career path with a firm mind that I was only going to work in Colorado to the exclusion of any other state, I would have missed some superb resume-building experiences, great cultural opportunities and many wonderful new friends that were made in the three states we lived in prior to making it to Colorado.

Things To Do Before You Graduate checklist

_____ Decide what I want to do when I grow up! (Before I graduate!)

_____ Grades are very important – pay attention to them!

_____ Seek internships for the summers between my college semesters. They are a way to open the employment door.

_____ Don't be a know-it-all!

_____ Differentiate myself as a candidate…there are many who are seeking the same opportunity I am, and differentiation is good.

_____ Do not fear networking – it is the most effective tool to use for job seeking.

_____ Don't unnecessarily gate or restrict my opportunities. Be open to the brave new world out there – I can live and work about any place for a few years.

5 Plan Your Work, Work Your Plan

By failing to prepare, you are preparing to fail.
– Benjamin Franklin

Many years ago when I was early in my corporate career, I transferred with AT&T from Salt Lake City, Utah to Basking Ridge, New Jersey (talk about a culture shock!). My department was on half of one floor, and another department was on the other half. A few weeks after I arrived, the employees of the other department were summoned to a 5:00pm, mandatory all-hands meeting. They were all informed they were losing their jobs and they had sixty days to find a job.

Even though it wasn't my organization, it felt like a blow to my mid-section. I had just moved my family 2,200 miles cross country. I knew no one. All my networks were back in Utah. What would I do if that happened to me and my organization? What would I do?

I mulled and worried about that for several weeks. Then one day as I was driving home thinking (brooding!) about it, the thought occurred to me: "If it happens to you, you'll go out and get another job. You're good at what you do, you have a good skill set and experience. You'll be fine." And that was it – I ceased worrying about it. So how does this apply to you as a new graduate? Well…remember those US Department of Labor statistics I provided in the first chapter? If not, here's a refresher:

- in 2014, new Bachelor's degree grads could expect 8.5% unemployment and 16.8% underemployment;

- nearly half (44%) of college grads won't find work that requires the degree they earned;

- salaries that 50% of recent grads will earn will be between $25,000 and $45,000;

- the true unemployment / underemployment rate is someplace between 15% and 25% (notwithstanding the numbers the government joyously announces each month!).

Notwithstanding this daunting set of statistics, you can and will find an opportunity. It may take some hard work, savvy searching and an understanding of the task ahead of you. But as you read the pages of this book, you should set yourself in a better position to achieve your career goals.

So far, I have shared a little information with you that may feel somewhat daunting – negative stereotypes, high unemployment rates for recent graduates, high percentage of recent graduates who cannot find work in the field in which they have their degree, etc. BUT – please don't get discouraged! Have faith in yourself. You have a lot going for you…you have a degree – which proves you can start and finish something of worth and value. And – if you think finding work in this economy is difficult, you are leaps and bounds ahead of those who are searching who have no degree.

> **I am good at what I do. I will get a job.**

Like me – you need to realize that you have a lot to offer employers. Yes, there are hurdles to overcome out there, but by now you've learned that you can overcome almost anything. So if you are one of the hundreds of thousands of recent graduates looking for work, have confidence you will find a job. It may be difficult, but you will beat this.

One of the most important tools you'll have in your job search arsenal is your attitude. Do whatever it takes to be positive. But also realize that in today's economy, you may be looking for a while, so prepare to be in this for the long haul. At the same time, don't dawdle in getting your resume out there.

I adopted the attitude that the very next job for which I applied would be *The One* that ended my unemployment. That meant I had to work hard, and not let any grass grow under my job-hunting feet.

So, what steps should you take to begin your job search? Read on and I'll tell you.

Resume

A good resume is critical to your job search. It should highlight your experience, skills, abilities and accomplishments. It should be squeaky clean – no typos, grammar difficulties, etc. But there's oh so much more – and that's why I have devoted an entire chapter to creating a resume that will present the most positive you. More on that in an upcoming chapter.

Cover Letter

Equally as critical as your resume, I believe, is a good cover letter. This element in your job search tool kit is so important I have provided a chapter for that also.

Get Organized

As you begin your job search, take time to organize your job search efforts. I can be a bit obsessive in my organization, yet I find organization helps me keep my mind uncluttered and on track.

One of the first things you'll find in your job search is that many jobs require you to interface with job search software – **applicant tracking systems** (ATS), they are called in the industry. These amorphous software packages serve as **gatekeepers** through which all applicants must pass. You'll have to complete an online application, upload your resume and cover letter, and probably answer multiple questions. You must take these seriously! It can be frustrating at times – applications in some of these ATS systems will take you about an hour to complete. But if you provide scant data, or rush through, you run the risk of having your resume sloughed aside and not considered – it won't even reach the hiring manager.

So the first thing I did was **create a spreadsheet** for my job hunt. It kept me focused, helped me plan my work and follow up. Initially the spreadsheet had only a few columns:

- date;
- name of company;
- title of position.

Over time, I expanded the columns to contain the following list of headings:
- date;
- interviews;
- name of Company;
- job board or networking contact through whom the job was found / referred by;
- title of position;
- salary range;
- contact;
- comments;
- login / password;
- website address.

Some of the headings are self-explanatory (date, job title, etc.), but here's just a word or two on several of the others:

Interviews
As I mentioned, I am obsessive about some things. I was interested in tracking my success – or lack thereof. So I created a column that tracked interviews. Whenever I got an interview with a company, I put a 1 in that column. At the end of the spread-

sheet I had a **total** column, so I could tell at a glance how many interviews I was getting. I only included an interview once for a company, even though I might have had several interviews at the company. I was more interested in how many companies I interviewed with, not the total number of interviews within a company. For example, I had seven interviews with 26 people at one company! But I only counted it as one interview in my spreadsheet.

There was more to this column than mere counting. It gave me an opportunity to see if there was a pattern developing. Was I more successful in getting interviews for positions that had a particular title, from a particular job board, etc.?

Job board where job was found / referred by

I was interested in seeing which job boards yielded the best results. I also wanted to know who had referred me to a particular company.

I ended up adding another tab on the spreadsheet listing all the job boards I was searching, with the numbers of jobs I found and interviews I received through each job board / referral. (More detail on that later in this chapter.)

Salary range

I found this was an area I was interested in tracking. Sometimes ATS systems required you to insert your salary expectations, and this was a helpful category. It was also helpful to know in case I got into salary negotiations.

Contact

I used this column to put the name and contact information for people important to this particular job – the person who referred me, hiring manager's name, recruiter's name, people with whom I interviewed at the company, etc.

Comments

I found I needed to make comments about who I had spoken with, what they said, etc. A typical entry was:

"**8/14** -- Heard from Susie Recruiter today at Acme Company. She wanted to set up an interview for 8/19. **8/19** – Interviewed with Harry Hiring Manager today. Felt the interview went well, wished I had researched the company a little more before the interview."

Login / password

As mentioned earlier, as you progress in your job search you will run into applicant tracking software. Many of them require logins and passwords. Unfortunately there are a half dozen variations (at least!) of what they will and will not accept as logins / passwords. Some require your e-mail address as a login, while others won't accept that. Some required passwords to be eight characters long and required a non-alpha character (?, !, *, etc.). In a very short amount of time I realized I couldn't mentally keep track of all the variations I had used, so I resorted to adding a column in my spreadsheet to capture the information.

Website address

When I found a job for which I was interested in applying, I cut and pasted the web address in this column. That way if I had questions later on about the position, I could go there with ease.

An important note on that last item: many of the jobs I applied for didn't yield interviews until five, six, eight weeks after my submission. Invariably, by the time I was contacted for an interview, job ads had expired and I couldn't find a copy of the job description any longer. So when I was called for an interview, I couldn't review the job description to plan my interview attack. I learned this very early in my job search, so **I added a tab in my spreadsheet titled** *Job Descriptions*. I cut and pasted each job description into this worksheet. I included a column with the company's name and listed the jobs alphabetically by company so it was easy to find later.

Networks

Although this is a difficult time in your life, this is not the time to keep to yourself. Tell everyone you know that you have graduated and you are looking for another.

This may be one of the most important moves you make as you begin your job search. We'll talk more about that in the **Network, Network, Network!** chapter.

Job Search Websites

An invaluable tool for your job search will be job search websites. Even though networking is the #1 way job seekers get jobs, you cannot afford to ignore the Internet for your job search, as nearly one in five jobs are found there by job seekers.

Generally speaking, job search websites can be placed into several categories:

- Career category websites (e.g., HR, engineering, teaching, government, graphic arts, etc.)
- Industry-specific websites
- General websites
- Aggregators
- Specific company websites

Let's look at each of these briefly:

Career Category websites

Most professions I know of have job websites specific to their industry or profession. In my case, as an HR professional, I identified a number of websites that focused on jobs in the Human Resources field. These included:

- Andrew Hudson's job list
- Colorado Human Resources Association
- SHRM

Industry-specific websites

At the time of my job search a few years ago, my most recent ten years of HR experience was in the legal industry, so I made certain I included several websites that represented law firms. I used one national website and several local websites. If you are not aware of websites specific to the industry you are interested in, there are several ways you can discover them. The first is to Google them. Go to the Google *Search* box and type: *(your industry) job websites*. Also, chat with the folks in your university's Career Center about what websites they would recommend. The department head at your university may also have some suggestions for you.

General Websites

Monster.com is one of the biggies. I have to admit that for years, I was not a fan of Monster.com, feeling it was too big and too general to be of use to me, either as an employer or as a job candidate. But I was pleasantly surprised at its value to me during my job hunt. Here are some other general websites you might consider as well:

- Careerbuilder.com
- Craigslist.com
- Jobing.com

Aggregator Websites

There are a number of excellent websites out there that I term as aggregators. They scan company and industry-specific websites for job openings, then pull the openings they find on all those other websites onto their website. So it's sort of one-stop shopping for job seekers. One of the best I found was Indeed.com. Here's a short list of aggregator websites I can recommend:

- Diversityjobs.com
- Flipdog.com
- Indeed.com
- Jobs2careers.com
- Juju.com
- Justjobs.com
- Simplyhired.com
- TopUSAjobs.com (subscription)
- Vast.com
- Yakaz.com
- Ziprecruiter.com

Specific Company Websites

Is there a company in your community for whom you would like to work? How about one of the **Top 50** or **Top 100 Companies to Work for in America**? Many of those very popular companies don't bother placing job openings any place but on their own website. I identified companies in my community I wanted to work with, and routinely checked their websites for openings for which I was qualified.

My success by website / source

Earlier in this chapter I promised to share the results of my job search – the number of jobs found and interviews I received by job board / networking referral. Here's the synopsis:

Source	Job Leads	# Interviews	%-age interviews / jobs
Andrew Hudson	4	0	0%
Career Builder	11	1	6%
Colorado HR Association	18	2	11%
Company websites	13	0	0%
Execunet	2	0	0%
TheLadders	21	5	24%
LinkedIn	4	1	25%
Monster.com	7	4	57%
National Association of Legal Administrators	3	0	0%
Networking	30	16	53%
Recruiters	7	2	29%
Society of Human Resource Managers	4	0	0%
Indeed.com	6	0	0%
Totals	**130**	**31**	**23.85%**

Here are a few quick notes about some of the above websites:

Career specialty or industry websites

Several of the websites above were specific to my HR career (SHRM, Colorado Human Resources Association, Andrew Hudson) or industry (National Association of Legal Administrators). You'll want to search out such websites if you are seeking a particular industry. TheLadders.com website is a website that only posts jobs whose starting salaries exceed $100,000. You'll note that Indeed.com was of very little use to me in my job search, but I believe had I found it earlier in my job search it would have been a very profitable website for me to use, and would probably have displaced at least several of the other job boards on my list above.

Recruiters

Occasionally I was either contacted by recruiters or found a job ad they had placed and submitted an application to them.

Company websites

Company websites were the websites of companies I thought would be great to work for, so decided to check their websites on a regular basis. Companies in this category included IBM, Google, Microsoft, Cisco, etc. As you can see, my efforts in this area yielded poor interview results (0 interviews), even though I found 13 jobs that matched my qualifications (10% of the jobs I submitted on). Regardless, if I were starting out a job search again, I would still check these websites.

As a recent graduate, or even as an undergrad, you should check out companies' websites to see if they have special opportunities for students / recent college grads. Just poking around a little bit while I was writing this chapter yielded many companies that have special hiring opportunities for interns and recent college grads, including Apple, Microsoft, AT&T, Cisco, Proctor & Gamble, Johnson & Johnson, etc. I was able to easily find these career websites for students at these companies by Googling *Working at Microsoft*, or *Student jobs at Apple*, etc. All of these and many other companies had links on their career websites specifically for *Students and Graduates*.

Networking

This category represents those jobs and interviews I got through the efforts of my network. You can see why I suggest networking so strongly – nearly 25% of the jobs for which I submitted applications came through this source, and I was successful in getting an interview over 53% of the time.

LinkedIn

LinkedIn proved to be a good, although not prolific, source for me. I joined a number of discussion groups for HR professionals. Occasionally another HR professional would post an opening in those discussion groups, such as:

> "I am seeking candidates for a Director of HR position at my company. Anyone interested should forward me their resume through LinkedIn."

I immediately had a contact within that company with whom to speak, so this was a great option for me. We'll talk more extensively about using LinkedIn and other social media websites in your job hunt in the **Social Networking** chapter.

Recruiters / Headhunters

I am often asked my opinion on recruiters / headhunters. My opinion is: use them. Seek them out. Let them help you find a job. But – do not just provide your name to a few headhunters and sit back and wait for your phone to ring. View them as one of many arrows in your job search quiver.

Headhunters typically focus on one industry – for example, I am personally acquainted with recruiters that focus on legal, healthcare, government, accounting, IT, etc. If, like me, your profession is one that can be practiced in multiple industries, then look for headhunters in a variety of industries.

Some headhunters focus on recent college graduates, and are worth talking to and working with. When working with recruiters, here are my **Recruiter Rules of Thumb**:

- Never use a recruiter who charges you money to place you;

- Check out the recruiter's website and see if it appears they represent recent graduates and students regularly;

- Beware of recruiters who offer other for-pay services – resume-writing, interview training, etc.;

- Help your recruiter – provide information they can use to place you (GPA, areas of study / focus, any experience you may have in the industry – PT jobs, internships, etc.);

- Ask for references – other students / recent graduates they have placed, and contact them – see how long it took for placement, any issues, things they liked, things they didn't like (this is a great networking opportunity, by the way!);

- Be honest with your recruiter – tell them the kinds of jobs you are looking for, your salary expectations, etc.;

- Regarding that last bullet point, listen to experienced recruiters, consider the input they give you regarding the kinds of companies that may be interested in you, starting salaries you can expect, etc.;

- Be wary of recruiters that throw you at every job opening out there – whether it's an industry or profession you want or not;

- Differentiate yourself in a good way – if you have something as a candidate that helps you stand out above the crowd – be sure and share it;

- As mentioned above, do not rely solely on recruiters – sign on with a recruiter, but continue your job search using other means.

Use recruiters but continue searching.

Set a Schedule

Okay, you have garnered all the tools at your disposal for your job hunt: resume, cover letter, networks of friends and associates, job search websites, and perhaps even a few headhunters. What next?

Your job, my young friend, is to find a job. You must treat your search as a job – you should put in 40 hours a week job hunting.

"What?!" You may ask. "How can I possibly job hunt 40 hours a week?" Well, the answer is simple. If you are doing it right, I believe you'll find that 40 hours each week will be barely enough to do all you need to do. Following is a sample week's job-search schedule that worked for me. Here is a typical schedule that you should repeat Monday through Friday:

8:00am to 11:00am – Search job websites, apply for any jobs that are of interest.

11:00am to noon – research companies you are interested in / have applied to. Try to find the hiring manager at the company. Company websites, calls to HR departments, networking contacts, etc. can all help with this.

Noon to 1:00pm – Lunch

1:00pm to 5:00pm – work your network – contact members of your network via e-mail or telephone. See if they know anyone at the companies where you have applied.

By following this schedule, you'll put in a minimum of 40 hours each week. Some days may be a little shorter, while others will be longer.

You may be one of those people that prefer to have the same schedule each day. If that's the case, by all means, do it that way: set yourself a schedule and follow it every day, day in and day out. I found that altering the schedule kept it interesting to me, and I didn't get into a rut.

Print off your schedule and post it, especially if you are doing your job-hunt activities at different times each day. If you are doing the same schedule each day, you needn't print your schedule and post it (provided you can remember it!).

With any luck at all, you will only have to follow your schedule for a very short time.

Now, if you're still in college, just finishing up, then obviously you cannot devote 40 hours each week to job hunting. And that's fine – there are only so many hours in a week. But you should set aside a healthy number of hours each week and reserve them for your job search.

Networking Groups

I found networking groups to be valuable to me in my job search. I joined several. One of them was a group of business men that belonged to my church. The first Tuesday of each month, about sixty of us met at a restaurant in the Denver metro area for lunch. Before lunch began, each of us stood and introduced ourselves. In the group were employers as well as those seeking employment. My introduction was simple and to the point:

> Hi, my name is Dan Quillen. I was recently laid off from my position as the Director of Human Resources at one of the largest law firms in Colorado. I have nearly 20 years of progressively more responsible Human Resources experience. I also have an MBA and am SPHR certified – sort of a CPA for Human Resources professionals. I am seeking a position as a Director or Vice President of Human Resources.

Others in the group introduced themselves with the name of their company and the position they held there. Frequently, one of those individuals would finish by saying, "Dan (or Tom, Bill, Sam, etc.) – my company has an opening you might be interested in – let's talk after lunch." I got a number of leads and a few interviews through this networking group.

I joined other networking groups as well, but the group sponsored by my church was the most valuable resource for me: they offered a resume class, a job interviewing class, and a job search class that shared various resources for job seekers.

It would be well worth your time to seek out and join networking groups, both those consisting primarily of job seekers as well as those consisting of a mix of job seekers and employed individuals. Work with the Career Center at your university to find networking groups; they will be a great resource for you.

Are there any networking groups in my area for students and recent grads?

Stay Busy

While most books about how to get a job will contain information about resumes, interviews, etc., I believe this bit of advice may not be found in any other job-finding book. I could be wrong, but think not.

Stay busy. Chances are you are going from a fairly rigid academic schedule to having lots of time to search for work. Be cautious – leaks in your schedule add up. Here were some of the things I did and didn't do during the months I was job hunting:

Things not to do

No daytime TV! I know myself, and know I can be a bit of a couch potato. I like movies and TV shows, as no doubt many of you do too. Because I knew it would be a temptation and a great time waster, I decided I would not watch any TV until 5:00pm at the earliest.

Not only do I write books, but like most authors, I like to read them – books are my friends. I decided I would not read any books between 8:00am and 5:00pm.

PLAN YOUR WORK, WORK YOUR PLAN

Things to Do

One of the best things I did was begin and continue an exercise program. Exercise is an excellent stress release, and I am sorry to tell you, but you are likely to experience stress during your time of unemployment.

I believe keeping busy will help you stay positive, and not sit around brooding or fretting about your situation. As you make and keep yourself busy doing productive things, you'll find the days do not drag, you'll be able to stay focused on your job search, and you'll feel productive. Depression is something you must constantly guard against.

Here is an important thought about keeping busy: **Keep your pipeline full of resumes and applications**. My job search lasted five and a half months. I soon noticed a pattern in my job hunt: most job interviews I received were either within two to three days of my submission, or five to six weeks after my submission. If you take a week off today, you may notice a week to ten days without an interview five or six weeks from now.

Prior to my unemployment I had arranged to visit an out of-town daughter and her family (actually, the visit was to see my grandchildren, and their parents were there too). Since the trip was already paid for, I opted to continue with the trip.

However, it wasn't a vacation -- I loaded all my information – resume, resume template, cover letter template, job search matrix, etc. on a laptop and headed for Chicago. Even though I was out of town, I wasn't on vacation. I still carved out significant portions of the day to conduct my job search. While there, in fact, I was contacted by a recruiter as well as set up several interviews.

So – keep that pipeline filled.

Plan Your Work, Work Your Plan checklist

_____ I am good – I will find a job!

_____ Resumes and cover letters are critical tools to be used in my job search.

_____ Organize my work; be methodical in my job search.

_____ Keep track of information about each job I apply for.

_____ Set a job search schedule and follow it.

_____ Use recruiters in my job search, but don't depend on them exclusively.

_____ Do not overlook the value of networking in my job search. I need to get comfortable with reaching out to my network.

Stay Positive

A positive attitude causes a chain reaction of positive thoughts, events and outcomes. It is a catalyst and it sparks extraordinary results.
– Wade Boggs

As you begin your job search – whether you begin while you're still in school or after you've graduated, if the time begins to stretch longer than you had hoped, it is important for you to keep your spirits up – to remain positive. As days extend into weeks, and weeks into months, you're liable to experience a wide range of emotions: shock, denial, self-isolation, anger, remorse, guilt, panic, depression, resignation, acceptance, building, optimism and elation. These are normal emotions, so don't be surprised when they sneak up on you and bite you.

These emotions aren't necessarily sequential, and you might leap ahead (to optimism and elation when you get an interview) or fall back (to resignation or panic when you hear you didn't get the job).

I have several friends who have been unemployed for long periods of time – years. Based on my working with them, I'd say these emotions are emotions each of them has experienced at one time or another in their job hunt.

I am by nature a very optimistic person, so I didn't experience some of the more difficult emotions listed here: depression and panic. But I did find myself needing to fight many of the other negative emotions.

So – be prepared for a wide range of feelings, and map a strategy to deal with the difficult situation you are facing.

You have already started doing that through the pages of this book. You are taking the first steps to placing yourself in the Land of the Employed: you're learning how to attack the challenge of finding work as a recent college graduate during a time when unemployment and underemployment is stiff for college grads.

I think one of your most valuable tools in your job hunt will be the ability to remain positive. Hundreds of books and articles have been written on the power of positive thinking, and you need to believe every one of them!

I have developed ten keys to staying positive during this trying time in your life. Let's see if you agree with them:

Key #1 – Keep Busy
One of the best things you can do to ward off depression is to keep busy. Prepare for battle, launch your resumes and cover letters into the great unknown at an unprecedented pace. Don't fire without targets, and don't fire ill-prepared ammunition. You need to plan your attack, prepare your weapons (your resume and cover letter) and identify companies for whom you are qualified to work. Plan how you will get resume screeners to put your resume in the *Call-for-an-Interview* pile.

Key #2 – Start an Exercise Program
Exercise is a great tool to battle depression. Select a time during the day that you will exercise, and stick to that schedule. Some people are morning people, and early mornings are a great time to exercise. However – you have to know yourself well. I know, for example, that any exercise program I start in the early morning hours is doomed to failure. I am one of those people that, if I was the one making the rules, I would say early morning meetings would be held at 10:00am or 10:30am in the morning. 5:00 only occurs once a day on my clock, and it is followed shortly thereafter by sunset.

I'd suggest exercising at least five, if not six days per week. I am a big believer in Sunday being a day of rest, and that makes sense for exercising my muscles too. The exercise I chose was to walk daily, Monday through Saturday.

Key #3 – Change Your Mindset

Surprisingly, this was one of the more difficult aspects of the job search for me. Prior to my lay off, we were pretty comfortable financially. We could buy things more or less at whim (within reason, of course. We couldn't, for example, buy the Dodgers when they were for sale…). I am a book fiend, and buy many books each year. Twenty minutes on Amazon.com and I could easily drop $200 or more, and this sometimes happened several times each month. I found I could no longer do that – I needed to shepherd my resources. I became a coupon clipper for the first time in my life.

This was a hard adjustment to make. Frankly, it was probably a good adjustment to make, as on a monthly basis, we were seeing hundreds of dollars slip out of our budget for non-essential items. Once I finally got my mindset changed, it was easy to do. But the first little while it was difficult.

As a college student, you may not need to do this – I know many college students are living pretty Spartan lives, so maybe your mindset is already there.

Key #4 – Marshal Your Resources

Financially, you should take stock and determine what resources are available to you. What cash reserves do you have? What revenues are coming in and what expenses demand payment? In a severe pinch, could a family member help out?

Are there expenses you can do without? Our home phone, internet and cable TV bill is close to $200 per month. We have cell phones, so we could certainly do without the cable TV and our home phone. That would save us a chunk of change. (We'd still need our Internet for job searching.) Do you have similar expenses? Are there corners you can cut? I have a friend who lost his job in May, and immediately sold his ski boat. He figured if he waited until the end of the water skiing season, he might be unable to sell the boat, or if he was able to sell it, he'd have to take less money for it. He traded in his wife's BMW for a car that was still functional but much less expensive. He economized.

You may want to look for something part-time to do to make ends meet. If you do that, be careful not to accept so many hours that you cannot conduct an effective job search. I've a friend who worked part-time for a moving company during his period of unemployment, and that allowed him the flexibility to work around the times he had set for his job search.

We stopped going out to eat. Whereas we were going out to eat once or twice a week, we curtailed that expense and saved plenty. Again – as a recent college student, perhaps this is not going to be an issue for you.

Key #5 – Remember: Millions of Americans ...
Whether you are a college student or recent graduate, if you are unemployed in America, you share that stage with millions of Americans. As we discussed before, for political reasons, the government reports only a portion of the unemployed in their official unemployment numbers each month...the others they assume have given up job hunting, so they don't include them in those official unemployment figures. I suspect that may be correct for some, but truly believe most of those millions should be counted as unemployed. Regardless – a LOT of people are out of work right now, many of them through no fault of their own. Recent grads are included in those numbers...at least for a few months. If after three and a half months after your graduation you are still unable to find a job, then perhaps you can feel some satisfaction knowing the government doesn't consider you as unemployed.

While the saying goes, *misery loves company*, that's not my point. My point is that you have not been singled out as the only recent graduate having a difficult time finding a job. Keep the proper perspective: you and millions of other outstanding people – top performers, bright (even brilliant) people, innovators, hard workers, etc., are looking for their first career job. Okay, that's a fact. But don't dwell on the difficulties facing you in finding a job that you miss opportunities that may be open to you.

Key #6 – Don't Be a Victim

I think this is an important consideration. Don't waste your time blaming others for any difficulties you face in finding a job, wondering how on earth you can't find a job with the degree you have in your back pocket. I had a young friend, a recent college grad from a reputable school, one well-respected in our community, who

struggled mightily to find a job. After a time, she became convinced the problem was the university from which she graduated – the degree just wasn't worth anything. Sometimes that kind of negative thinking comes through in your cover letters, and often even in your job interviews. You cannot afford for that to happen.

Here's something important to keep in mind – companies that hire recent graduates do so with full knowledge that you don't have years and years of experience – so don't worry about that.

Key #7 – Set a Schedule

In the previous chapter, I wrote about setting a schedule and sticking to it. I reiterate that counsel here. I think if you are busy doing something productive with your time, the time will pass quickly, you won't sit around and brood or worry about your unemployed status, etc. Your job now is to find a job, and you should set a schedule and stick to it.

Key #8 – Get Plenty of Sleep

Getting plenty of sleep is important, as it will help you deal with the depression and self-defeating doubts that might creep in occasionally. One of the best bits of advice I received at the time of my lay-off was to get good, consistent sleep. Occasionally I stayed up way later than normal, but generally speaking, I was in bed most nights by 10:00pm and arose most mornings by 7:00am.

Key #9 – Prepare for the Long Haul

At the time of this writing, our economy is improving somewhat. But it is so fragile. An unexpected jobs report, a lower earnings (or loss) report of a Fortune 200 company, unrest in the Middle East and a host of other such calamities (or risks of calamity) can cause the economy to reel and step back a few paces.

Set your expectations appropriately, or you risk being disappointed. If you feel you'll be employed in two weeks, then I am afraid you may be disappointed. The key is to work as though you will be able to be employed in two weeks if you work hard, but be realistic in the expectation that it may take longer than that to become employed. (And rejoice if it takes just two weeks!)

Key #10 – Build in Some Entertainment

All work and no play makes Jack (and Jill) a dull boy (and girl). Make some time for yourself. Make time for your family – remember, everyone who loves you and in particular those who live under the same roof is sharing this experience with you, in one way or another. If you are a recent graduate with a spouse / significant other, or are living with your parents, they are all part of your job search.

When I told my mother I had been laid off, she said, referring to our two oldest children: "Oh, this would be a great time for you to go visit Katie in Chicago and Michael in Portland." I said yes, if it weren't for the need to be cautious with our monies at this time. Of course it would be unwise to take that round-the-world trip you've always wanted to take at the conclusion of your college career, or pack up and head for Disney World.

But, depending on where you live, a drive in the mountains or a trip to the nearby beach to see the sunset are inexpensive ways to spend time together and get out of the house. Perhaps a trip to the mall as a family, looking for the most outrageous window display you can find would keep everyone's spirits up. Or just a picnic in the park. We like Redbox movies – even on a tightened-belt budget we feel we can afford to rent a movie or two at Redbox.

Whatever it takes, don't allow yourself to slip into the doldrums.

Key #11 – Hang in There!

Finally, hang in there. This time in your life will be over sooner than you think. Hopefully in the future as you look back on this experience, you can do so with introspection and insight, perhaps even fondness. It is easy to be professional when everything is going your way. But real professionalism manifests itself during adversity.

You'll note I said I had ten keys, but provided eleven. Well, I am a firm believer in not over-committing, and in always providing more than promised …

Stay Positive checklist

_____ I am in good company – I am not the only recent graduate having a difficult time finding a job in this New Economy.

_____ Keep busy.

_____ Start an exercise program – endorphins are a great way to battle anxiety.

_____ Don't be a victim.

_____ Set – and follow – a schedule.

_____ Hang in there!

Your Resume / Some Experience

Emphasize your strengths on your resume, in your cover letters and in your interviews. It may sound obvious, but you'd be surprised how many people simply list everything they've ever done.
– Marcus Buckingham

Since this is a book on getting a job, you know there will be a chapter on resumes. I have reviewed tens of thousands of resumes during my career. I have screened them for my own hires, as well as for other hiring managers. As I have reviewed resumes, one thing has been painfully clear – too many people do not spend enough time on their resumes, and it costs them the job for which I am screening. This could be one of the most important things you attend to during your job search. There are other important elements to your job hunt, but many of them will not be able to be used if you don't get in the door, and your resume is one of the primary ways you'll open that all-important door.

Some experts say you have less than thirty seconds to grab a resume reviewer's attention with your resume. Personally, this is how much (or should I say how little!) time I spend reviewing resumes:

- first review = 3 to 5 seconds;
- second review (if you pass the first review) = 15 seconds.

That may seem difficult to believe, but HR departments and managers can determine in a moment or two whether they are interested in a candidate.

Now, I am going to share with you a method to craft your resume that should increase your potential to land interviews (and a job!) **300% to 500%** over what your chances will be if you don't follow my recommendations.

When I was searching for a job after my layoff in mid-2011, I submitted 130 applications. Those 130 applications yielded 31 job interviews for me – nearly a 24% hit rate. Having been out of the job searching business for many years, that seemed pretty anemic to me. However, as I spoke with other job seekers and met with networking groups, they were all amazed at my level of success. Leaders of the networks of which I was a member claimed their group was averaging more like 3% to 5% hit rates (one interview for every 20 to 35 resumes / applications submitted), and they all wondered how I was achieving such a high success rate with my resume. They asked that I present classes on what magic I had that made my resumes more appealing and successful. (Note: Those presentations eventually led to the writing of a number of books, including this one.)

Before we get to the magic I used to win interviews as a result of my resumes, let's talk about a few things that apply specifically to students and recent graduates. Here are a few general things to consider:

1. You must differentiate yourself from other new graduates. Any experience you have that is relevant to the position needs to be highlighted on your resume.

2. Make sure the relative skills you do have (notwithstanding lack of extensive experience) stand out on your resume through a *Skills* section or well-worded *Summary* statement.

3. If you have any experience that relates to the job at hand, be sure you include it in a manner that the reviewing individual will be able to find easily.

4. Tailor your resume for every job you apply for. Scan the job ad for the job you are applying to, searching for what it is the employer is seeking, and if you have experience in those areas, make sure you include it on your resume.

5. Is there anything you've done that might look good on your resume in an Awards or Honors section? Were you Employee of the Month? President of your sorority? Raised funds for orphaned children in Africa? Received a scholarship for a portion or all of your schooling? Make sure you include it on your resume. (See #1 above – differentiate yourself.)

I think now is a good time to introduce you to the three primary resume formats with which you should be familiar, the pros and cons of each, and help you determine which will be best for your needs. The three primary resume formats are:

- Chronological
- Functional
- Chronological / Functional hybrid

Chronological resumes are those you may be most familiar with – they have been and are the standard resume format for the business world. Having said that, you may assume that is the resume format you should use. Maybe, but maybe not. While it is the most common format out there today, I do not think it is as effective for students and recent graduates if they do not have experience, particularly in the field you are seeking employment.

Chronological resumes list jobs and experience in a reverse chronological manner – so that your most recent (and presumably most relevant) jobs will be listed first. Let's take a look at a few bullet points from my personal resume – for an example:

W. DANIEL QUILLEN, SPHR

Street Address, City, State & Zip Code   303-555-1212   wdanelquillen@gmail.com

PROFESSIONAL EXPERIENCE

Director of Human Resources   **2001 to 2011**
Holme Roberts & Owen LLP, Denver, CO

- Protected the firm from lawsuits by handling all disciplinary actions up to and including terminations using sound employment law practices. Over the course of ten years and 200+ terminations, there were no lawsuits filed against the firm for employment actions.

• Used competency modeling expertise to assess required skills for positions, and identified skill gaps within the work force. Training curricula developed to address deficiencies within the various work groups, resulting in a more efficient and skilled work force.

• Developed, launched and administered a voluntary staff development program designed to enhance staff skills and enrich their work experience. Ongoing classes supported and attended by over 90% of staff. Hailed as a significant success by firm management.

• Effectively managed all health benefits for the firm. During a five-year period, negotiated over $2,000,000 in savings for the firm while maintaining one of the best benefits packages in the market (excellent benefits, low deductibles, moderate premiums, etc.).

Director of Legal Recruiting   2005 to 2007
Holme Roberts & Owen LLP, Denver, CO

• Directed the recruiting and hiring of attorneys and paralegals into the firm. Over a two-year period, brought 44 associates and 11 paralegals into the firm. This allowed the firm to increase revenues, lower its per-attorney overhead and increase partner profits.

• Established national contracts with several recruiters, negotiating lower rates than were normally offered. Savings for the firm were substantial, as rates were typically 33% lower than normal.

Senior Human Resources Manager   1998 to 2001
Avaya/Lucent Technologies, Westiminster, CO

• Due to success in complex HR situations, was asked to provide HR support to 1,400 Avaya Labs (formerly Bell Labs) scientists, a large department with significant complexity to their HR work (organizational development, recruiting, retention, compensation, etc.). Earned Exceeded and Far Exceeded ratings and performance bonuses for work with this group.

• Designed a recruiting strategy for our business unit, aimed at recruiting and selecting only "A" players into our business. Allowed us to bring in more qualified employees, reducing turnover and increasing efficiency. Business unit strategy became the model for corporate-wide recruiting.

Note that, with little preamble, I launch right into my experience, beginning with my most recent experience and moving backwards from there. The end of the resume might contain things like any awards and honors I have received through the years, and information about my education. **Pros and cons of chronological resumes include**:

Pros

> • Hiring managers and HR professionals can immediately see the experience I have had, and how it relates to the job for which they are interviewing;

> • The progression from present day backwards allows the hiring manager to see the progress I have made in my career – very positive if I have received promotions as I progressed in my career;

> • Hiring managers can quickly see the job titles I have held, and this may help them determine that my experience fits their needs;

> • Hiring managers can scan the bullet points under each of my jobs to see if I have the experience and skill to do the job for which s/he is hiring.

Cons

> • This format requires the hiring manager to search through my resume for key words and experiences to see if they match what s/he is looking for in a candidate;

> • If you do not have much experience, it makes for a pretty short, non-informative resume;

> • Without taking the time to read each bullet point, it's not immediately obvious what my skillset is, or what my strengths are.

Functional resumes allow you to highlight your skills, experience and interest, even if you do not have a great deal of actual experience. It is a very effective resume for recent graduates who do not have much experience beyond book learning and possibly an internship.

Functional resumes list your skills and knowledge (even if only gained through coursework) and that is the focus of the resume. Your experience – if, indeed, you have any in that area – is often relegated to the end of the resume in a very short section that just lists the companies and jobs you have held, along with the dates the positions were held. Let's take a look at a sample functional resume:

AURIANNA ST. PIERRE

www.LinkedIn.com/in/astpierre   720-555-1212   astpierre@email.com

PROFESSIONAL SUMMARY

- Rising business professional with human resources experience and training

- Creative problem solver with respect for precedent, but also willing to try new things.

- Enthusiastic team player who adds value to the team and supports team members.

- Multi-lingual (English, Spanish, German) professional with customer service focus.

- Proficient in the Microsoft Office suite of software (Word, Excel, Access, PowerPoint).

- Intellectually curious, driven-to-learn professional.

PROFESSIONAL SKILLS AND ACCOMPLISHMENTS

Human Resources

- Provided HR support for seventy seasonal workers at a restaurant / dude ranch.

- Investigated employee complaints, including sexual harassment, hostile workplace,

- Americans with Disabilities Act (ADA) accommodations; all complaints resolved without legal action.

• Updated employee handbook, adding updated chapters on Fair Labor Standards Act (FLSA), ADA and Family Medical Leave Act (FMLA).

• Interviewed and hired approximately 30% of staff for summer and fall season; no performance issues among these employees.

Marketing and Communications

• Recommended the company begin a client newsletter to attract return visits from clients; company owners estimated newsletter was responsible for 23% increase in business over a six-month period ($50,000 to $75,000 increase in sales).

• Served as editor and writer for client newsletter; newsletter delivered electronically to 3,000 clients every two weeks.

• Developed employee reward and recognition program, celebrating top performance among company employees. Morale increased, and employee attrition dropped to almost 5% compared to 20% attrition in previous years.

Customer Service

• Taught customer service classes to new and returning employees.

• Rewarded prestigious Employee of the Month award four times at three different employers.

• Interacted with internal and external customers, striving for excellence in each exchange.

PROFESSIONAL EXPERIENCE

Human Resources Intern, Big Bob's Dude Ranch and Eatery, Salina, KS May to October 2015

HR Manager, CollegeWorks Clothing, Rexburg, Idaho, January to July 2015

Landscaper, Arnold's Landscaping, Idaho Falls, Idaho July to October 2014

Cashier, AMC Theaters, Aurora, Colorado, 2008 to 2011

AWARDS AND HONORS

- Named *Employee of the Month* four different times with three different companies.

- One of the youngest crew leaders ever appointed by my company.

- Named shift lead after only three months on the job.

- Graduated magna cum laude with 3.8 GPA.

EDUCATION

Bachelor of Science, Business Administration with Human Resources specialization, 3.8 GPA, magna cum laude

Brigham Young University, Provo, Utah

Unlike the chronological resume, the functional resume begins with the skills and knowledge this candidate has. Note that this resume begins with a *Professional Profile* – a section that allows the candidate to share some good general information about themselves that may be of interest to employers. The next section, *Professional Skills and Accomplishments*, allows the candidate to highlight those skills and experiences s/he has that are relevant to the job for which they are applying. **Pros and cons of functional resumes include**:

Pros

- The skills and capabilities of the candidate are quickly on display for hiring managers – no need to search through the resume for those skills;

- Especially for those with little experience, functional resumes allow you to highlight your strengths and knowledge, while taking the spotlight off your lack of experience.

Cons

> • Functional resumes are not good resumes for experienced professionals – they allow experienced candidates to more easily hide gaps in employment;

> • Many hiring managers are wary of functional resumes, particularly with experienced candidates. With recent graduates, however, most hiring managers understand perfectly that you won't have much experience, so this format is very effective.

Chronological / functional hybrid (Chronolotional? Funcological?) resumes are a wonderful combination of the chronological and functional resume format, combining the strengths of each.

Chronological / functional resumes start out listing strengths and skills at the top of the resume, like a functional resume, and then list your work experience in reverse chronological order. That is followed by other things like accomplishments and honors, education, etc. Let's take a look at a chronological / functional resume for my fictional / composite recent graduate friend, Ms. St. Pierre:

AURIANNA ST. PIERRE

www.LinkedIn.com/in/astpierre   720-555-1212   astpierre@email.com

PROFESSIONAL SUMMARY

Rising business professional with Human Resources experience and studies. Strong, creative team player looking to make a contribution to the bottom line. Fluency in multiple languages (English, Spanish and German, with a smattering of Italian) provides an additional dimension that allows great flexibility. Strengths include:

• **Human Resources**	• **Team Player**	• **MS Office**
• **Compensation**	• **Problem Solver**	• **Creativity**
• **HR Compliance**	• **Customer Service**	• **Self Starter**

PROFESSIONAL EXPERIENCE

Human Resources Intern   **May to October 2015**
Big Bob's Dude Ranch and Eatery, Salina, KS

- Provided HR support for seventy seasonal and twenty full-time workers at restaurant / dude ranch.

- Investigated employee complaints, including sexual harassment, hostile workplace, Americans with Disabilities Act (ADA) accommodations; all complaints resolved without legal action.

- Interviewed and hired approximately 30% of staff for summer and fall season; no performance issues among these employees.

HR Manager   **January to July 2015**
CollegeWorks Clothing, Rexburg, Idaho

- Updated employee handbook, adding updated chapters on Fair Labor Standards Act (FLSA), ADA and Family Medical Leave Act (FMLA). Allowed company to be in compliance with federal labor laws.

- Recommended the company begin a client newsletter to attract return visits from clients; company owners estimated newsletter was responsible for 23% increase in business over a six-month period ($50,000 to $75,000 increase in sales).

- Served as editor and writer for client newsletter; newsletter delivered electronically to 3,000 clients every two weeks.

Landscaper   **July to October 2014**
Arnold's Landscaping, Idaho Falls, Idaho

- Provided residential and commercial landscape support, including planting trees and shrubs, laying sod and placing flagstones.

- Responsible for landscape sales; led all sales for the company each month, averaging 122% of quota (never below 100%).

Cashier   **2008 to 2011**
AMC Theaters, Aurora, Colorado

- Provided customer service to moviegoers to ensure their viewing experience was as positive as possible.

• Recognized four times as *Employee of the Month* for outstanding customer service effort.

AWARDS AND HONORS

• Named *Employee of the Month* with three different companies.

• One of the youngest crew leaders ever appointed by my company.

• Named shift lead after only three months on the job.

• Graduated magna cum laude with 3.8 GPA.

EDUCATION

Bachelor of Science, Business Administration with Human Resources specialization, 3.8 GPA, magna cum laude

Brigham Young University, Provo, Utah

The chronological / functional resume format is by far the most well known in business circles today. It begins with a short professional summary, expands to a list of skills and knowledge, and then provides employers with a list of experiences the candidate has had at several jobs. **Pros and cons of chronological / functional resumes include**:

Pros

> • Within the first few inches of the resume, hiring managers can see at a glance the skills and knowledge the candidate has, both through the short *Professional Summary* paragraph and the list of skills and knowledge provided immediately thereafter.

> • Hiring managers can scan the job titles held by the candidate, and see quickly whether or not they have the experience that will allow them to do the job for which they are hiring.

Cons

> • Obviously, this is a difficult resume format to use if you do not have experience.

> • If there are gaps in your employment, they will be accentuated by this resume format. Let me hasten to point out that for college students or recent graduates, there is no concern from hiring managers about gaps in work history – they understand your first job is your school work.

So – which resume format should you use? The choice is up to you. Look at your experience, skills and knowledge, and determine which will accentuate the positives in your candidacy.

There were several reasons I wanted to provide these three resume format examples. First, I think they provide you with good insights into the resume options you have available to you. Second, I have provided copies of those resumes for three additional reasons. First, throughout the rest of this chapter, I will use these resumes to illustrate a number of points I wish to make about resumes. Second, later on in this chapter I will show you two versions of one of Aurianna's resumes – one of which is much more effective than the other. The final reason I give these three examples is in case you want to copy one of the formats (not the content or experience, please!) to use in your own resume.

Okay – let's get started. Let's begin with some general comments about resumes.

Proofreading

A point I cannot stress forcefully enough: it is absolutely critical that your resume have no typos and no grammar or tense errors. These can sink a resume as quickly as lack of experience, poor grades, etc. While one typo might be acceptable (we all make mistakes!), by the time I get to the second or third typo in a resume, I am pretty much done with it. Every job I know of requires attention to detail (okay, maybe you can blur the lines a bit if you are an impressionistic painter), and typos in a resume are just plain unacceptable to most business people.

Microsoft Word provides a wonderful spell checker – be sure and use it! However, be careful of words that a spell checker won't pick up:

- hear / here

- there / their / they're

- its / it's (learn the difference between these two!)

- affect / effect (if you aren't dead certain when to use these two words, don't use either!)

- to / too / two

- stray letters. Did you know that if you leave a letter all by itself in a sentence, spell check doesn't flag it as a spelling error? For example:

The cat was n the barn.

Watch out for what I call **restructuring errors**. Word processing software is great and allows you to make rapid revisions. But sometimes, you leave "orphan words" in your sentences. For example:

Original sentence:

I have been responsible for leading a team of highly effective benefits and payroll employees.

Intended revision:

I led a team of highly effective benefits and payroll employees.

Final version (with orphans included – **bolding added** to highlight the orphans):

I **have been** led a team of highly effective benefits and payroll employees.

I cannot stress enough that you must read and re-read your resume, making sure there are no typos, grammar issues, etc. And then, once you have read it several times, read it again! Take your time. If you are a writer, the rule of thumb is to review your completed manuscript seven times before you send it to a publisher. I consider myself a pretty good proofreader, and I am always amazed at how many issues I pick up during readings six and seven – especially toward the end of the manuscript.

After you have done your review, have someone whose opinion you trust review your resume with a critical eye – "yes" men and women are not helpful. I have found that spouses, significant others, parents and siblings are *not* good reviewers – they love you and don't apply the critical eye you need. If you've done a good job, your reviewer probably won't pick anything up. However, they'll be more likely to notice little things that affect your resume: spacing that isn't even throughout the resume, some bullet points use periods and some do not, etc.

One caution – if you ask someone to review your resume, don't be offended by their recommendations. You don't have to incorporate them if you're not comfortable, but don't be offended – they are trying to help you.

I have reviewed resumes and cover letters for years for many people. A number of years' ago I ran into an old high school classmate at a retail store. After we exchanged greetings and caught up with one another, he explained he had lost his career job and was just working at this retailer until he could get back into his career field. He said he had submitted his resume for many jobs, but was never able to get an interview. When he learned I was in HR, he asked me to review his resume. I was happy to do so, and I am sad to say, it was a veritable train wreck: typos, grammar and tense difficulties, etc., etc. It was, quite frankly, a horrific resume -- one of the worst I have ever reviewed. No wonder he wasn't getting any interest from those companies with which he had submitted his resume. I drafted an e-mail with all my suggestions; I spent hours on it, giving him suggestions, even providing him with a draft template for a new resume.

I sent it off to him and heard nothing. Finally after about two months he contacted me and told me how incredibly offended he had been at my criticism of his resume (even though I was as gentle as I could be). He said he sulked for a long time, then finally came to the realization that I really had his best interests at heart, and finally realized how much he appreciated my review.

So – don't be like my old classmate. Be appreciative of the efforts your reviewers make in your behalf. Be gracious even though you may not agree with their suggestions.

Proofreading hint: I found by personal experience that I am a *terrible* proofreader on screen. I have learned that to be effective in my proofreading, I need to print out hard copy and review it. I don't understand why; guess that's just one of my (many) quirks!

Proofread carefully!

Acronyms and Jargon

Be cautious in using jargon and acronyms. When I began my career, I was in sales for Mountain Bell Telephone. One of my co-workers received a work order (called a *bluie* by employees because it was on blue paper) indicating that a customer wanted a visit (PV – which stood for Premises Visit) for a business line (a 1FB) on their telephone system (KTS). So, bluie in hand, my co-worker called the customer and said:

> "Hi, this is Rod from Mountain Bell, and I have a bluie here that says you need a PV to discuss getting a 1FB on your KTS."

Understandably, the customer had no idea what my work associate was saying!

I share that story to help you understand you must be careful with the acronyms you use in your resume. If the acronyms you use are common to your industry, you may be okay – a hiring manager is likely to know what you mean. But a recruiter or human resources person may not. If you are going to be using the acronym once in your resume, I'd suggest spelling it out. If it will likely appear numerous times in your resume, then I'd suggest using this format the first time:

> Senior Professional in Human Resources (SPHR)

and then you can simply use the acronym throughout the rest of your resume.

Length

If you have read any of my other books (*Get a Job!*, *The Perfect Resume* or *The Perfect Interview*), you'll note that I am adamant that your resume must be no more than two pages, because as a reviewer, I have no patience for three-page tomes, much less those that are longer than that.

That said, please don't take that to mean you *must* have a two-page resume! As a college student or recent graduate, it is very possible (even probable) that your resume will only be one page, or perhaps a page and a half. And that's just fine. As I've discussed before, hiring managers understand recent college graduates won't have extensive resumes yet.

Formatting

I've a few words about the font size I recommend:

> Many hiring managers are Boomers – and their eyesight isn't what it used to be. The font size in your resume should be no smaller than 12-point font; 13-point font is better, 11-point is terrible.

> Many hiring managers are Boomers – and their eyesight isn't what it used to

be. The font size in your resume should be no smaller than 12-point font; 13-point font is better, 11-point is terrible.

Many hiring managers are Boomers – and their eyesight isn't what it used to be. The font size in your resume should be no smaller than 12-point font; 13-point font is better, 11-point is terrible.

Can you see the difference in those identical sentences? The first is written in 13-point font, the second is 12-point, and the third is 10-point. In an effort to get more information in their resumes (and to get to two pages!), many individuals resort to 11- or even 10-point font, and it is a mistake – it is hard to read, and may get your resume cast aside rather than stress the eyes of your (potential) hiring manager. Whenever possible, use 12- or 13-font, never 10 or 11. Generally speaking, I try to use 12-point font for most of the body of my resume, and 13-point font for my section headings.

Hyphens

May I just say a word or two about hyphens? Even though it probably won't matter too much in your resume since most people don't know how to use hyphens, it will make me feel better.

When two words are used together to modify another word, they should be hyphenated, even if they might not normally be hyphenated. Here's an example:

The movie was first rate.

That was a first-rate movie.

In the first sentence, using those two words without a hyphen is just fine. But in the second sentence, the two together form an adjective that modifies the movie – it was a *first-rate* movie. But wait, in the first sentence we say the movie is first rate – doesn't that phrase modify the movie? Yes, however the rule says you only use the hyphen if it comes before the word.

The exception to this rule is if the first word used ends in –ly:

I was responsible for leading a team of *highly effective* benefits employees.

Since words ending with –ly are actually adverbs, you do not need to use a hyphen with the second word.

Finally, numbers from twenty-one to ninety-nine should be hyphenated (excluding, of course, twenty, thirty, forty, etc.).

As I say, most individuals don't know how to properly use hyphens, so I don't think it will matter if you don't use them correctly in your resume. However, if you are applying for a position as an English teacher, then missing hyphens might be the kiss of death. I always appreciate a candidate who uses hyphens correctly, but I don't consider it a typo when not used.

Thanks. Now I feel better. My wife would tell you that by inserting this section, my OCD is showing. (Except for me, it should be *CDO*, because everyone knows letters should always be listed in alphabetical order….)

Font Style
I prefer to see resumes in **Times New Roman** rather than Arial or **Calibri**. Times New Roman seems more business-like, more professional to me. I will admit that a great number of resumes I have reviewed for technical positions (IT professionals, engineers, etc.) seem to either be in Arial or Calibri. They do have a much more… *technical* look than Times New Roman, so I suppose they would be okay for those types of positions.

Having said that, I don't believe using any of those fonts would be a deal killer. You must make certain, however, that whichever font you use does not negatively impact the readability of your resume. There are some pretty fun and crazy fonts available out there, but I would say that's not how you want to make your resume stand out. Lucinda Handwriting is pretty cool looking, but I think it is a little more difficult to read than ... Times New Roman.

Photographs

I have to admit, through the years I have gotten few resumes with pictures of the applicant attached – I can count the number on one hand, in fact. That's good. Unless you are applying for a job as a model, actor or actress, on-screen television role, etc., you should not attach your photograph (no matter how handsome / pretty you are!).

Formatting

Earlier, I mentioned I would provide you with several versions of the same resume for you to consider. Here is a **slightly shortened version of Aurianna's chronological / functional** resume again:

AURIANNA ST. PIERRE

www.LinkedIn.com/in/astpierre   720-555-1212   astpierre@email.com

PROFESSIONAL SUMMARY

Rising business professional with Human Resources experience and studies. Strong, creative team player looking to make a contribution to the bottom line. Fluency in multiple languages (English, Spanish and German, with a smattering of Italian) provides an additional dimension that allows great flexibility. Strengths include:

• **Human Resources**	• **Team Player**	• **MS Office**
• **Compensation**	• **Problem Solver**	• **Creativity**
• **HR Compliance**	• **Customer Service**	• **Self Starter**

PROFESSIONAL EXPERIENCE

Human Resources Intern   **May to October 2015**
Big Bob's Dude Ranch and Eatery, Salina, KS

- Provided HR support for seventy seasonal and twenty full-time workers at restaurant / dude ranch.

- Investigated employee complaints, including sexual harassment, hostile workplace, Americans with Disabilities Act (ADA) accommodations; all complaints resolved without legal action.

HR Manager   **January to July 2015**
CollegeWorks Clothing, Rexburg, Idaho

- Updated employee handbook, adding updated chapters on Fair Labor Standards Act (FLSA), ADA and Family Medical Leave Act (FMLA). Allowed company to be in compliance with federal labor laws.

- Recommended the company begin a client newsletter to attract return visits from clients; company owners estimated newsletter was responsible for 23% increase in business over a six-month period ($50,000 to $75,000 increase in sales).

Landscaper   **July to October 2014**
Arnold's Landscaping, Idaho Falls, Idaho

- Provided residential and commercial landscape support, including planting trees and shrubs, laying sod and placing flagstones.

Cashier   **2008 to 2011**
AMC Theaters, Aurora, Colorado

- Recognized four times as *Employee of the Month* for outstanding customer service effort.

AWARDS AND HONORS

- Named *Employee of the Month* with three different companies.

- One of the youngest crew leaders ever appointed by my company.

- Named shift lead after only three months on the job.

- Graduated magna cum laude with 3.8 GPA.

EDUCATION

Bachelor of Science, Business Administration with Human Resources specialization, 3.8 GPA, magna cum laude

Brigham Young University, Provo, Utah

And here is that same version – with very little special formatting:

Aurianna St. Pierre

www.LinkedIn.com/in/astpierre   720-555-1212   astpierre@email.com

Professional Summary

Rising business professional with Human Resources experience and studies. Strong, creative team player looking to make a contribution to the bottom line. Fluency in multiple languages (English, Spanish and German, with a smattering of Italian) provides an additional dimension that allows great flexibility. Strengths include Human Resources, creativity, customer service, compensation, HR compliance, team player, problem solver, MS Office, self starter.

Professional Experience

Human Resources Intern   May to October 2015
Big Bob's Dude Ranch and Eatery, Salina, KS

- Provided HR support for seventy seasonal and twenty full-time workers at restaurant / dude ranch.

- Investigated employee complaints, including sexual harassment, hostile workplace, Americans with Disabilities Act (ADA) accommodations; all complaints resolved without legal action.

HR Manager   January to July 2015
CollegeWorks Clothing, Rexburg, Idaho

- Updated employee handbook, adding updated chapters on Fair Labor Standards Act (FLSA), ADA and Family Medical Leave Act (FMLA). Allowed company to be in compliance with federal labor laws.

- Recommended the company begin a client newsletter to attract return visits from clients; company owners estimated newsletter was responsible for 23% increase in business over a six-month period ($50,000 to $75,000 increase in sales).

Landscaper   July to October 2014
Arnold's Landscaping, Idaho Falls, Idaho

> • Provided residential and commercial landscape support, including planting trees and shrubs, laying sod and placing flagstones.

Cashier   2008 to 2011
AMC Theaters, Aurora, Colorado

> • Recognized four times as Employee of the Month for outstanding customer service effort.

Awards & Honors
• Named Employee of the Month with three different companies.
• One of the youngest crew leaders ever appointed by my company.
• Named shift lead after only three months on the job.
• Graduated magna cum laude with 3.8 GPA.

Education
Bachelor of Science, Business Administration with Human Resources specialization, 3.8 GPA, magna cum laude

Brigham Young University, Provo, Utah

Look at both of those versions of Aurianna's resume critically. Each resume is identical – same content, same layout, etc. Without taking the time to review each resume, without taking the time to read for content, I think you will agree that the first one – the one with the formatting, is the most professional looking of the two, and the one that will have a better chance of standing out among the dozens or hundreds of resumes in the stack sitting on a hiring manager's desk. Don't believe me? Copy both versions of the resume and lay them side-by-side; without spending time on the content of either resume, you decide which looks more professional.

Resume Sections

We've covered some of the general information about resumes. Now let's review Aurianna's resume one section at a time – and I will comment on each individual section, giving you my thoughts on each.

AURIANNA ST. PIERRE

www.LinkedIn.com/in/astpierre   720-555-1212   astpierre@email.com

Nothing fancy here. I prefer to have my name centered and in larger font than the rest of the resume. I have seen resumes that have the person's name either left- or right-justified, and those are fine too. You do, however, want balance in your resume. So try putting your name in all three places and see which you like best, which feels best.

There is some debate about whether or not you should put your home address on your resume. A few years ago my son asked me to review his resume. He had left his address off, and I suggested he include it. Said he: "But Dad, my college careers office said to leave it off." So he left it off.

A few weeks later, he shared with me that he had received a call from a company to which he had applied, asking for his address – seems they wanted to send him some information about the company. I smiled and graciously acknowledged how interesting that was.

Then a few months later I was making a presentation about resumes to one of the networking groups I belonged to. It was a mixed group, consisting of job seekers and hiring managers. Several of the hiring managers weighed in and said they had dismissed resumes because when they looked at the address, they decided the person wouldn't be willing to make the commute. A rich, valuable and interesting discussion ensued among the group members on the topic. About 50% favored including the home address, and the other 50% felt it was more a liability than an asset to have it on the resume.

So I leave it to you, dear reader, whether you want to include your address or not. However – you should strongly consider putting in its place the URL of your LinkedIn profile. Before you do so – make sure your profile is up to date and professional looking. 75% of recruiters report using LinkedIn to learn more about potential candidates, and you might as well make it easy for them by including your LinkedIn profile on your resume.

Be sure and provide your phone number – whether or not you provide your home number, your cell number, or both is up to you. I have mixed emotions about that. I list only my home phone because I am just not happy with the overall quality of cell phones. Often there is the omnipresent background static / noise that interferes with the quality, and dropped calls are still too frequent (can you recall the last time your home phone dropped a call?!).

Regardless of whether you use your home phone or your cell number, make sure there is a professional-sounding greeting. We have all heard the cutesy two- or three-year-old greeting on home answering messages, and while that delights grandma and grandpa, it doesn't present much of a first impression to potential hiring managers or HR departments. Now I can't imagine anyone would dismiss you as a candidate for that reason, but still it begins the first impression.

I don't believe your greeting needs to be as formal and professional as that which you would have at your office. A more generic greeting is fine:

> "Hi! You've reached Aurianna St. Pierre. I'm unable to answer the phone right now, but if you'll leave your name, number and a message, I'll call you back as soon as I can."

Stay away from greetings like: "*You* called *me* – you know what to do." I am not a big fan of music for the first ten seconds of the recording either.

Bottom line on greetings – remember, you are seeking work, and you wish to present the best first impression possible on all contacts with potential employers.

Always – always – include your e-mail address. Once while I was working in my previous job, I asked a large group of my peers whether they called or e-mailed applicants to set up interviews. I was moderately surprised to learn that about 75% used e-mail and 25% called. Personally, I always prefer e-mail – sometimes calls go unanswered, you leave a message, the applicant calls and misses you, etc. I prefer an e-mail – it's quick, clean, and can be responded to at any time of the day or night. Here is a strong recommendation regarding your e-mail address: ditch the silly, cutesy, goofy e-mail addresses for your job hunt.

A few years ago my 110-year-old staid and stodgy law firm was advertising for an assistant controller. I received a number of resumes, and narrowed it down to a half dozen. I prepared to send e-mails to the applicants inviting them to come in for an interview, when I ran across this e-mail address of one of the finalists:

One_Hot_Woman@_____.com

Amused, I shared the information with my boss. He laughed and said, "Well, we're not hiring her, but I want to interview her!" We both laughed about it.

As it turned out, we didn't end up interviewing her, as an internal candidate stepped up and we promoted her.

Along those lines, here are a few e-mail addresses I have actually seen on resumes, presumably seeking serious employment:

- LazyBrain@XXXX.com
- I_Will_Do_Anything@_____.com
- ThePartyAnimal@_____.com

Seriously – I don't know what these people were thinking. E-mail addresses are cheap – they are free! Go get one that is much more professional, even if you only use it for your job search.

Also, **be certain you check your e-mail frequently** – at least daily, preferably several times throughout the day. Recently, at my current employer, we were filling the position of a benefits administrator. We screened the resumes and identified five individuals we wanted to interview. On a Monday afternoon I sent e-mails to the top five candidates, inviting them in for an interview three days hence – on Thursday. Most of the candidates responded within hours of the request. As the day of the interviews approached, I still hadn't heard from one of the candidates. I reached out again on Wednesday afternoon and offered him an interview slot on either Thursday or Friday. He never responded.

We went forward with our interviews. The last candidate we interviewed was exceptional, so we offered her the position on Thursday afternoon.

On Friday afternoon, the candidate who hadn't responded e-mailed to say he had been away from his e-mail for a few days and would love to interview with us. I had to tell him I was sorry, but the position had already been offered to another candidate. Don't miss out on interviews because you don't check your e-mail frequently!

As mentioned earlier, people are busier in the American workplace than they have ever been. Sometimes hiring managers will try to bring candidates in between several meetings or projects that are due, and sometimes short notice of interview opportunities is given. I am embarrassed to say that I have e-mailed candidates hoping they would be available the next day for an interview. If you only check your e-mail once a day or just several times a week, you may very well miss out on a golden opportunity! Note: I do cut candidates some slack if they are not available the next day, but not everyone does!

Okay, now for the next section:

PROFESSIONAL SUMMARY

Rising business professional with Human Resources experience and studies. Strong, creative team player looking to make a contribution to the bottom line. Fluency in multiple languages (English, Spanish and German, with a smattering of Italian) provides an additional dimension that allows great flexibility. Strengths include:

- **Human Resources**
- **Compensation**
- **HR Compliance**
- **Creativity**

- **Team Player**
- **Problem Solver**
- **Customer Service**
- **Self Starter**

- **MS Office**

You'll note that in three sentences I have provided some critical phrases that summarize what kind of candidate Aurianna is:

- Rising HR professional (with HR experience and university studies)
- Team player looking to contribute to the bottom line
- Creative
- [a] Multi-lingual

Tailoring

Now we are getting to the meat of resume preparation and writing. It is crucial to your success in finding a job in today's New Economy. In fact, I feel so strongly about this that I am going to bold and center it:

You must tailor every resume for every job for which you apply.

Hiring managers in today's work environment are so busy with their day-to-day responsibilities that it is hard for them to slow down and review the hundreds of resumes they receive for every opening. Consequently, they have employed resources they never used before to help them. These sources include applications software designed to automatically screen out the least-qualified candidates (more on this later), Human Resources departments and possibly others like administrative assistants, etc.

When I graduated from college, and for many years thereafter, a squeaky-clean resume set job seekers out from the crowd. But those days of having one good, generic resume for every job are long gone – one size doesn't fit all! You must tailor your resume for every single job you are seeking. Even though as a recent college graduate you don't have extensive experience, you must accentuate that which you do have, especially the skills, knowledge and experience you have that is relevant to the job for which you are applying.

But how do you do that? In five easy steps:

1. Print the job ad.

2. Read it from beginning to end, making mental (or literal) notes about the skills and experience they are seeking.

3. Go back to the beginning and read again, this time circling or highlighting those skills and experiences that are important to the hiring manager – those that are listed in the job description.

4. Now, take the list of highlighted items and make a priority list. You will highlight the Top 9 or 10 skills, knowledge and experience they are seeking.

5. Using the list from item #4, begin tailoring your resume to fit the job description.

Let me give you an example. While writing this chapter, I went to Monster.com and in the Search box, I entered: *entry-level marketing*. Following is the job ad for an entry-level marketing / promotions / management position that came up (one of many, I might add!):

****

Looking for a NEW Career with Advancement Opportunities?
Stop Looking! Start Here!

ABOUT US:

_____ has a responsibility to create a **greater awareness for our clients** by using a cutting edge **promotional marketing method** to bring their products or services directly to the community. We strive to reach **goals** not only for our company, but our clients, customers and staff as well. Our clientele consists of Fortune 500 Companies, National Retail Stores and Clients in the Entertainment Industry.

_____ OPPORTUNITIES:

We are rapidly expanding! *We are currently welcoming individuals with little or no marketing or advertising experience to join our company*. We have exciting positions for anyone who wants to get his or her "foot-in-the-door" in the world of **business marketing** and have excellent "ground floor" positions for individuals who want to grow quickly to a position of GENERAL MANAGEMENT. Qualified candidates will be trained in the areas of: **Promotional Sales** (one on one sales interaction with customers), **Event Marketing**, **Advertising** and **Campaign Management**.

TO APPLY:

All openings are FULL-TIME and need to be filled A.S.A.P.!!

There is **no experience necessary**. If you are a looking for experience, or someone who is aggressively pursuing a change in careers, please APPLY!

The ideal candidates will possess a "second-to-none" **work ethic**, strong desire to advance and grow with the company and an unbelievable **positive business attitude**. Our office is comprised of very **driven, self-motivated individuals** that are very serious about their careers. This is a perfect opportunity for someone trying to get their "foot-in-the-door" in the marketing field.

THERE IS NO GRAPHIC DESIGN, NO TELESALES, NO CUBICLES, NO DOOR TO DOOR!

Candidates with **NO EXPERIENCE**, students and grads welcome. If you have a **willingness to learn**, a **positive attitude**, and **customer service skills** you can start immediately.

****

In the body of the job description, I have **bolded** the following key elements of this job, which I gleaned from the job description:

- **Customer Service** (awareness for our clients)
- Goal oriented
- **Marketing**
- **Advertising**
- Sales
- Event marketing
- Campaign management
- Strong work ethic
- Positive business attitude
- Driven
- Self motivated
- Willingness to learn
- **Positive attitude**

So – out of this baker's dozen skills, do you think some of them apply to you? Scan that list; are there any that you think are most important to the company? The ones I have bolded were mentioned more than once in the job ad: **Customer Service**, **Marketing**, **Advertising** and **Positive attitude**. Have you ever worked on a job where you had customers? Remember that customers could be the general public, but they could also be individuals in other departments or organizations that depend on your output to do their jobs. As a recent graduate, do you have a positive attitude about life? Marketing and advertising may be a little more difficult to show as a skill, however, if you took a marketing and/or advertising class, you could consider yourself as having experience / knowledge of those areas.

But even if you don't have the hard skills like marketing and advertising (sales, event marketing, campaign management), you almost certainly have at least a few of the other "soft" skills they list: goal-oriented (you graduated from college, didn't you?!), strong work ethic (no one sat on your shoulder pushing you to do your homework, go to class, etc!), willingness to learn (what have you been doing the last four+ years?!), self motivated, driven, etc.

Once you identify nine skills / knowledge you have which is relevant to the job for which you are applying, those become the nine skills / strengths you list in this section:

• Customer Service	• Driven	• Goal Oriented
• Advertising	• Marketing	• Strong Work Ethic
• Positive Attitude	• Self Motivated	• Sales

Note that the first four – Customer service, marketing, advertising and positive attitude – are listed in the first column and the top of the second column. This is because these are the first areas managers / HR professionals will be looking when they are looking at your skills and knowledge. Make it easy on them to see you have the skills and knowledge they are looking for!

If the job ad lists fewer than nine skills / knowledge areas, or you do not have all those areas for which they are advertising, then lead with those skills and knowledge you do have, then complete the list of nine with other skills you have that seem relevant to the job.

Again, let me say that if you wish to be successful in finding a job in this difficult New Economy:

You must tailor every resume for every job for which you apply.

As a reminder – prioritize the bullet points you use for your *Professional Summary* section. From your reading of the job description, decide which are the most important skills the company is seeking. The first three should be in Column #1, and the next two most critical skills should be the first skill listed in each of the other two columns. This part of crafting your resume is more art than science. Usually the top three to five skills are generally pretty easy to determine.

Also – and this is important – use the company's language! If they use the term *Talent Acquisition* instead of *Recruiting*, you should use *Talent Acquisition*. In a later chapter, we'll address applications software, and you'll see how critical it is to have the right terms in your resume.

Moving on to the next section:

PROFESSIONAL EXPERIENCE

Human Resources Intern   **May to October 2015**
Big Bob's Dude Ranch and Eatery, Salina, KS

- Provided HR support for seventy seasonal and twenty full-time workers at restaurant / dude ranch.

- Investigated employee complaints, including sexual harassment, hostile workplace, Americans with Disabilities Act (ADA) accommodations; all complaints resolved without legal action.
- Interviewed and hired approximately 30% of staff for summer and fall season; no performance issues among these employees.

HR Manager   **January to July 2015**
CollegeWorks Clothing, Rexburg, Idaho

- Updated employee handbook, adding updated chapters on Fair Labor Standards Act (FLSA), ADA and Family Medical Leave Act (FMLA). Allowed company to be in compliance with federal labor laws.

- Recommended the company begin a client newsletter to attract return visits from clients; company owners estimated newsletter was responsible for 23% increase in business over a six-month period ($50,000 to $75,000 increase in sales).

- Served as editor and writer for client newsletter; newsletter delivered electronically to 3,000 clients every two weeks.

Landscaper   **July to October 2014**
Arnold's Landscaping, Idaho Falls, Idaho

> • Provided residential and commercial landscape support, including planting trees and shrubs, laying sod and placing flagstones.

> • Responsible for landscape sales; led all sales for the company each month, averaging 122% of quota (never below 100%).

Cashier   **2008 to 2011**
AMC Theaters, Aurora, Colorado

> • Provided customer service to moviegoers to ensure their viewing experience was as positive as possible.

> • Recognized as *Employee of the Month* for outstanding customer service effort.

The *Professional Experience* section of your resume should begin with your most recent position and work backwards.

Unless you have worked for one of the 800-pound gorillas of Corporate America – IBM, Microsoft, Apple, Google, etc. – your future employer will most likely be interested in your job title, not in the company for which you worked. Therefore, your title should be on the first line, and your company should be on the second line:

Human Resources Intern   May to October 2015
Big Bob's Dude Ranch and Eatery, Salina, KS

instead of:

Big Bob's Dude Ranch and Eatery, Salina, KS   May to October 2015
Human Resources Intern

Consider whether the company name might set you apart for applications within your industry. Perhaps the company you worked for is only a 75-pound chimpanzee in Corporate America, but is the 800-pound gorilla in your industry. For example, my 250-attorney, 500-employee law firm was tiny in the Corporate American jungle, but it was one of the largest law firms in the western United States. While I generally led with my title, whenever I was applying for a position within the legal community, I led with my firm name. Compared with the other things we'll discuss in this chapter, this is a minor point, so I wouldn't spend an inordinate amount of time deciding on which way to go, but it's a part of the bigger resume picture.

Unless you have had a succession of short-term jobs, listing your length of service with a company should be done in years. Anything under two-ish years should include the months:

- December 2007 – August 2009

A listing of 2007 – 2009 could be as little as 13 months (December 2007 to January 2009) or as long as 24 months (January 2007 to December 2009). Of course, if you have had a series of short-term jobs, you may wish to only list the years.

As a college student or recent graduate, you may have a series of short-term jobs – summer jobs. If that's the case, don't fear putting them down and using the months you worked there. These job tenures:

- June to August 2015
- July to September 2014
- June to August 2013
- June to August 2012

speak volumes to hiring managers – they tell them that you worked during your summer vacations. And all the better if you went back to the same company – that shows you were well enough thought of to be hired again – valuable information for hiring managers!

Each of the bullet points under your *Professional Experience* section should be gleaned from the job description and to the extent possible should **match the nine bullet points** you have in your *Professional Summary* section. This section may not be long enough to have bullet points for every one of the nine skills bullet points, but you should hit most of them, and certainly you should address those you feel are the most critical for this position.

In other words, if you can show you have been utilizing / demonstrating the skills and knowledge you identified from the job ad, it will speak well for your resume and experience.

Your goal with your nine bullet points and the bullet points under each of your jobs (in particular your latest job!) is to have whoever is reviewing your resume say to themselves and others: "Wow! This candidate has been doing **exactly** the job we are looking for!" *Don't make them pore over your resume trying to figure out if something you have done in the past matches what they are looking for.* Make it easy for them and tailor your resume to exactly what they are looking for.

Here's a caution – you can only do this if you have actually had experience in each of these areas. Don't puff your resume or exaggerate your accomplishments or activities. That's not honest. But do present your true self in the best possible way! But remember – as a recent college graduate, your experience / knowledge may be limited to those courses you took in the area that's important to the potential employer. So – you took a marketing class and gained some knowledge, and you also took an advertising class and gained knowledge that way. While not literal experience, it can still be listed. During your interview, if the question comes up, you will need to tell the hiring manager that your experience is limited to the knowledge you gained through the particular classes you took.

Just as important as tailoring your resume, do all you can to **make sure as many of your bullet points as possible has an accomplishment**! You say you were responsible for recruiting? So? Maybe you were the *absolute worst* recruiter to ever do the job. Can you think of something that was impressive, some accomplishment you can nevertheless highlight that shows you weren't just some mediocre performer? Sometimes it's difficult to come up with accomplishments, but you must try.

Let's look at Aurianna's resume. Here are some entries that listed not only her responsibilities, but made an effort to **identify accomplishments**; some accomplishments are more quantifiable than others, but nonetheless, she made the effort:

> • Provided HR support for seventy seasonal and twenty full-time workers at restaurant / dude ranch.

> • Investigated employee complaints, including sexual harassment, hostile workplace, Americans with Disabilities Act (ADA) accommodations; **all complaints resolved without legal action**.

> • Interviewed and hired approximately 30% of staff for summer and fall season; **no performance issues among these employees**.

> • Updated employee handbook, adding updated chapters on Fair Labor Standards Act (FLSA), ADA and Family Medical Leave Act (FMLA). **Allowed company to be in compliance with federal labor laws**.

> • Recommended the company begin a client newsletter to attract return visits from clients; company owners estimated newsletter **was responsible for 23% increase in business over a six-month period ($50,000 to $75,000 increase in sales)**.

As an HR professional, some of my major responsibilities are to ensure that my company isn't sued because of poor employment practices (discrimination, unlawful discharge, etc.) and to manage our benefits package. Here are two of the bullet points I used on my resume to highlight those areas of my responsibility, without accomplishments:

- Handled all disciplinary actions up to and including terminations using sound employment law practices.

- Managed all health benefits for the firm, including plan design, negotiation and determining premiums.

And now here they are with **accomplishments added** (note: the bolding is for your sake, I did not bold these in my resume):

- **Protected the firm from lawsuits** by handling all disciplinary actions up to and including terminations using sound employment law practices. **Over the course of ten years and 200+ terminations, there were no lawsuits filed against the firm for employment actions**.

- **Effectively** managed all health benefits for the firm, including plan design, negotiation and determining premiums. **From 2006 through 2011, negotiated over $2,000,000 in savings for the firm while maintaining one of the best benefits packages in our market (excellent benefits, low deductibles, moderate premiums, etc.)**.

During a number of the job interviews I had, the hiring manager specifically mentioned the accomplishments associated with these two areas of responsibility and asked me to relate more about how I did that.

Some responsibilities lend themselves more to accomplishment identification. Are you in sales? How did you do? Did you consistently exceed your sales objective, year after year? Were you 150% of quota? Were you given a difficult territory and you were able to increase sales by 30% over previous years? Did you earn any salesman of the month / quarter / year awards? Tell your story!

Following is one of the responsibilities for which I had difficulty finding an accomplishment:

    • Developed, launched and administered a voluntary staff development program designed to enhance staff skills and enrich their work experience.

That's not a task that lends itself to quantification. However, I was determined to show an accomplishment in each of my areas of responsibility, so here is what I came up with:

    • Developed, launched and administered a voluntary staff development program designed to enhance staff skills and enrich their work experience. **Ongoing classes supported and attended by over 90% of staff. Hailed as a significant success by firm management**.

I was able to quantify it – 90% of the staff supported this voluntary program – and that management called it a significant success.

Now is not the time (nor during your job interview) to be modest. You have to toot your own horn a little bit. If you don't – the hiring manager won't know just how good you are. Most people I know don't like braggarts, but you must strike a balance between bragging and not mentioning your strengths and accomplishments due to humility.

This may seem like a lot of work. It is. But let me put it this way: You can apply for a job in five to ten minutes using a generic resume, and never hear back from the company, except perhaps one of their canned responses that says, "Thanks, but no thanks." Or – you can spend an hour or so sprucing up your resume and tailoring it

Include accomplishments in my resume.

to the specific job at hand, and increase your possibility of being interviewed four- or five-fold. The choice is yours…but what else are you doing with your time? What else is demanding your attention during these involuntary days off that are now part of your life? I happen to think tailoring each resume is a pretty good use of your time during this phase of your life.

And make no mistake about it – this will take effort! But, from personal experience I can tell you that as you get into the swing of things it gets easier. First, it gets easier because you are getting better at identifying the elements from the job postings that need to be highlighted in your resume. Second, if you follow my next suggestion, it will get even easier.

As I was beginning my job search, it didn't take long for me to realize that many of the job ads for the jobs I was seeking required the same things: experience in benefits, recruiting, employee relations and recognition, training, organizational development, etc. I found myself writing the same entries under my jobs over and over again, or trying to remember in which previous resume I had already included a particular skill or experience. I decided to get smart: I created a resume template. I called it *DQ resume template*. When I opened the template, it looked like my resume, except that it eventually grew to five pages. Included in it was a listing of all the "nine bullet points" items I had identified during my job search:

- **Recruiting**
- **Benefits expertise**
- **Legal compliance**
- **Employee relations**
- **Evaluations**
- **Multi-site HR**
- **International HR**
- **Strategy development**
- **Problem solver**
- **Succession planning**
- **Organizational design**
- **Leadership development**
- **Interpersonal skills**
- **Generalist skills**
- **Influencing skills**
- **Analytical skills**
- **Decision-maker**

- **Communication skills**
- **Benefits expertise**
- **COBRA, FMLA, HIPAA**
- **Mergers / acquisitions**
- **Performance management**

In addition – every time I ran across a new area for which I needed to develop a bullet point to be used under a particular job (along with accomplishments, of course!), I would develop it and put it in my template. By the end of my job search, I had thirty-five such items. I won't list all thirty-five, but here's a sampling:

• Protected the firm from lawsuits by handling all disciplinary actions up to and including terminations using sound employment law practices. Over the course of ten years and 200+ terminations, there were no lawsuits filed against the firm for employment actions.

• Investigated and resolved all employee complaints of hostile work place, gender discrimination, sexual harassment, EEOC claims, etc. Resolved all complaints satisfactorily for the complainant and the firm. During ten-year tenure, not one lawsuit was filed against the firm.

• Frequent changes within the firm required effective employee relations and interpersonal skills. Mergers, acquisitions, and recession-related changes in firm policy and guidelines all required extensive ability to inspire and retain employees. As demonstration of success in these areas, one retiring employee observed, "Dan put the *human* back in Human Resources."

• Led all staff and paralegal recruiting. Sourced, interviewed and hired candidates. Ensured candidates had required skills and cultural fit for the firm. Extremely low turn-over rate among new hires resulted in excellent client service and an efficient and productive work force.

• Effectively managed all health benefits for the firm. From 2006 through 2011, negotiated over $2,000,000 in savings for the firm while maintaining one of the best benefits packages in our market (excellent benefits, low deductibles, moderate premiums, etc.).

Note for a moment the first two bullet points. Basically they say the same thing, and I wouldn't use them in the same resume. However, the second one would be used if the job description said the company was looking specifically for someone who had experience in EEOC issues and complaints. The first one might be used if the job description indicated they were looking for someone with legal compliance background. While the items themselves are only slightly different, I used one or the other *based on what the hiring manager was seeking.*

As I was applying for jobs, tailoring my resume became easy, because I could just go to my template and select a pre-written item. The wording was already worked out, the accomplishment identified and – I had already scrubbed it for typos. All I had to do was cut and paste the item where it belonged on my resume.

Again, you ask: "Dan, this is an awful lot of work."

And I reply: "Yep."

There is a very good reason to do this. Remember – you have three to ten seconds to hook the resume reviewer. By completing your nine bullet points and including experiences that mirror those bullet points, you have a much greater chance of getting a second look, and eventually an interview.

As a college student or recent graduate, your resume template won't be as extensive as mine (probably!), but after you get the hang of it, you'll become more and more adept at identifying bullet points that will be relevant to the job you are applying for, and which match some experience or coursework you have had.

Let me make an important distinction here when it comes to tailoring your resume. **Do not cut sections of the job ad and paste them into your resume**. Hiring managers will see that and dismiss your resume as soon as they recognize what you have done (I would, anyway!). Use your own words to tailor your resume, not the company's job ad.

On to the next section:

AWARDS AND HONORS

- Named *Employee of the Month* four different times with three different companies.

- One of the youngest crew leaders ever appointed by my company.

- Named shift lead after only three months on the job.

- Graduated magna cum laude with 3.8 GPA.

The Awards and Honors section is a section I strongly recommend. It helps differentiate you from the crowd. So you were a cashier at a local movie theater – there are millions of them in America. Oh – you were designated *Employee of the Month* a couple of times? Were elected president of your sorority three years in a row? Tell that story! You can include your *Employee of the Month* award in the *Professional Experience* section as one of the bullet points, if you prefer, but I kind of like it pulled out and highlighted in a special section like this. If you have only one such element, then it probably doesn't warrant a separate section; but if you have several, you may want to consider putting them in an *Awards & Honors* section.

Use this section to highlight those activities you did that might be considered above and beyond the call of duty. Perhaps you were selected as your class representative at an important student-faculty committee determining new policies, or wrote a syllabus for a course that was adopted by your entire department, or you wrote articles for the student newsletter or website All these are activities and accomplishments you are proud of and set you apart from the unwashed masses – tell your story!

On to the next section:

EDUCATION

Bachelor of Science, Business Administration with Human Resources specialization, 3.8 GPA, magna cum laude

Brigham Young University, Provo, Utah

As with the *Professional Experience* section, unless you graduated from one of the top-tier schools in the nation – Harvard, Princeton, Stanford, Yale, and the like – lead with and bold your degree. Do not include your dates of graduation; that allows a screener to determine your approximate age. Some applications software asks for it, but usually allows you to continue in the application without inputting it. I think it's just a wise practice to exclude that whenever possible especially as you move further along in your career.

If you graduated with honors – Summa Cum Laude, Cum Laude, etc., -- include that. Similarly, if you had a high GPA – 3.9 or 4.0 – you should include that.

If you attended a branch of a school, be sure and identify the branch; for example:

- University of California Berkeley
- University of California Los Angeles
- BYU Idaho
- BYU Hawaii
- University of Nebraska Lincoln
- University of Nebraska Kearney
- University of Colorado
- University of Colorado – Colorado Springs

Sometimes there is no difference in the school campuses, sometimes there is. If there is – perhaps the main campus has a more prestigious reputation than your campus – don't try to pass yourself off as a graduate of the main campus. It's not honest, and a quick reference check or transcript requirement will indicate your dishonesty and may cost you your dream job.

Include the field in which you graduated and any minors or specializations you may have had, especially if they are relevant.

In recent years, I have seen a number of resumes that lead with their education section. My recommendation is not to do that, unless you are seeking a job as an attorney, educator or doctor. Leading with your education section is pretty standard format in the legal, education and medical industries (for doctors – not nurses, CNAs, LPNs, etc.).

Also, if you graduated from one of the top schools in the nation, you may want to lead with that section on your education.

What do you do if you left school without completing your degree, or are still in school (whether full-time or evenings)? I would show that information, and if you have one, put an estimated graduation date. Here is an example:

Candidate for Bachelor of Science in Business Administration, with Mathematics minor
University of Colorado (Boulder, CO) (estimated graduation date: 6/1/20XX)

If you started college and didn't finish, I would include that:

Candidate for Bachelor of Science in Business Administration, with Mathematics minor
University of Colorado (Boulder, CO) (completed five semesters)

While that last is not as strong as having completed your degree, it is still better than no college at all. And – go back and finish! Even if you have to do it one class at a time, do it!

If you have no college or perhaps only one semester, I would not include an education section in your resume. Do not put the high school you graduated from – it merely highlights that you didn't go to college. If you are a young person just beginning your career, either before or after you have attended college, see the *Are You Too Young for this Job?* chapter for a few hints and tips in this area.

If you have taken classes through your work or other venues, it is okay to add classes you think might be applicable to the position for which you are applying. If you do, limit it to those that are directly relevant. But don't take up valuable space in your resume just to include these classes. If, however, you get to the end of your resume and have space remaining, I think it is fine to include these classes in the *Education* section.

Sections Not Included

Perhaps as important as the sections to include in your resume, are the sections not to include. Here are a few:

Objective Statement. I am not a fan of *Objective* statements at the beginning of resumes. Are they wrong? I think not. But I prefer to see that information covered in the cover letter. And – I am always amused at those *Objective* statements that say something like: "I am seeking a position in the medical industry to utilize my skills and experience." In and of itself, there's nothing wrong with that, except that the job I have open isn't in the medical industry!

Personal. No offense, but I have absolutely no interest in your hobbies, marital status, volunteer work or other such personal tidbits of information. You were a Division 1A collegiate or professional athlete? I'll admit that's impressive to me, broken-down old athlete that I am. But I would prefer to see information like that in an *Awards / Honors* section, or in your cover letter.

Not long before I began writing this book, I reviewed a professional resume with the following *Personal* section:

> Married to Cindy, a ceramic artist and potter. We have two sons, Scott, a biologist and Anthony, a music teacher. My family and I enjoy swimming, biking, hiking, skiing, camping, climbing mountains, golf and most any outdoor activities. We also enjoy cultural experiences including art, music, and travel.

Now I am certain Cindy is a lovely woman, and Scott and Anthony are perfectly delightful children, but none of that is something I have the slightest bit of interest in as a hiring manager. Note: names in the above paragraph have been changed to protect the innocent!

The only exception I have run across in my review of thousands of resumes is one fellow's *Personal* section that included the fact that he had led a blind climber up Kilimanjaro and Mt. Everest. Now that is something I found impressive!

References Available Upon Request. I wish I had a dollar for every resume I have reviewed with that superfluous ditty appended at the end of a resume. That is assumed. I have yet to ask a candidate for their references and had them say, "No, I think not."

In Summary

A couple of closing thoughts on your resume:

I know we have taken a lot of time in this chapter speaking about your resume. But it is such an important part of your job search – really the first visible aspect thereof. Yes, there is preparation up front – organization, identifying networks, etc. – but this is a most critical step. The *Interview* chapter is pretty extensive too, since that's where you really get to shine and hopefully close the deal. But without a great resume, you may not even get an interview, even though you are the most qualified candidate. What a tragedy for you as well as for the company who would have hired you.

Your Resume checklist

_____ There are three standard resume formats: chronological, functional and chronological-functional hybrid.

_____ Decide which resume best represents my experience and skills.

_____ Make sure my e-mail address is professional. What message am I sending?

_____ I must tailor every resume for every job for which I apply.

_____ Use job ads to identify the skills and knowledge the hiring manager is seeking, and include them in my resume.

_____ Use accomplishments in my resume whenever and where ever possible.

_____ Do not include Objective statements, Personal sections, or References Available Upon Request sections.

_____ Be completely honest in my resume.

8 Your Resume / No Experience

A man who carries a cat by the tail learns something he can learn in no other way.
– Mark Twain

Thank you, Mr. Clemens for painting a vivid visual picture for us!

Perhaps as you have read through the pages of this book you have felt discouraged because you have no experience.

When I was in high school, my parents didn't want me to work during the school year. "Your job," they said, "is to do well in school." And so I didn't work during the school year. It meant I had to hustle out there to find a job when summer rolled around, because many of my peers were looking for the same kinds of jobs as I was. I was always successful in finding work, but some of friends were not so fortunate. Perhaps you used the same thought process while you were in college – you didn't work during the school year because you were laser-focused on doing well in your studies and earning a superior GPA. But at the end of the day, while you earned a 3.9 GPA and have no job, many of your peers with 3.4 GPAs are getting jobs because they have more experience than you (limited though their experience is).

What do you do about that?

You may have more experience than you think…

Don't limit your definition of experience to the jobs you have held...or in this case, the jobs you haven't held. I won't lie to you – it's best if you do have real-world work experience. But if you don't, don't just throw your hands up and give up.

In this chapter I will show you important ways to improve your resume and your job search overall if you have no work experience.

Consider your life for experiences that taught you leadership – employers like leadership skills, and there are a plethora of places you may have picked up that kind of experience. You were a boy scout or a girl scout? Did you have any leadership positions – patrol leader, treasurer, historian, scribe? Lacking job-related experience, list those.

You formed a club in college? Were team captain of the debate team in high school or college? Vice president of your high school's National Honor Society? Earned an academic scholarship? Tell your future employers about that.

Not everyone can be THE leader. So you weren't captain of your DECA club, but were a member of the team that took the state DECA title? Then tell that story – you were a member of a team that pulled together and meshed their diverse talents to win the DECA state title.

Have you done volunteer work in the field in which you are seeking a position? List it. Chances are since you are going into a particular field, you have had experience somehow related to it. You're going into Criminal Justice and did ride-alongs with police officers? List that. You're going into veterinary medicine and worked or volunteered in a kennel? Be sure and mention it. Hiring managers like to see you have an interest in a field long before seeking career employment in it.

Find an Internship
This may seem odd to say, but if you are lacking experience, one of the ways is to get it through an internship. Yes, you have graduated, but lacking any work-related

experience, you may find it difficult to find work, even if you put together a resume with non-work-related leadership experiences.

Haunt your university's Career Center and ask for their help. Explain your dilemma – while focusing successfully on your grades, you neglected to get any experience. They may know of companies that will look beyond the lack of experience, that will be more flexible than others might.

It may feel like you're stepping back – after all, aren't internships for those who haven't yet graduated?! You've got mountains of student debt and you need a job to begin chipping away at Mt. Everest. Yes, all that is true. But if you accept an internship – paid or not – you begin getting that oh-so-important item you need for your resume – experience.

It would be a terrible pill to have to swallow to accept an unpaid internship. However, paid or not, you will be gaining valuable experience – experience which will help you get work elsewhere.

Another word or two about internships. Internships are wonderful opportunities to get your foot in the door of a company, and to show them how good you can really be for them. But – make no mistake -- they are first and foremost a job interview – a very extended and in-depth job interview. The hiring company will be evaluating you and watching to see if you are the kind of employee they want to have at their company. Your work ethic – what time you show up to work, how late you stay, your availability for projects, are all considered and evaluated.

The quality of your work is also considered. They know you haven't got experience and can't be expected to know as much as employees who have worked there for years. But they recognize half-hearted efforts and sloppy work. All your work should be packaged as though you were presenting it to the toughest grading professor at your school. No typos, sentence fragments, incomplete thoughts, etc.

In a word (actually – in four words): **Take your internship seriously**.

Since you don't have years and years of experience, show what you do have. If a company is willing to hire new talent, you will be competing against others who have little or no experience also. Accentuate the positive!

Network

Earlier in this book I wrote about networking (remember the *Network, Network, Network!* chapter?). Networking is another way you can unlock the employment door when you have no formal work experience. Someone who knows you may be able to speak for you in a manner that will offset your lack of experience.

While writing this chapter, I attended an HR luncheon / education session. At the beginning of the meeting, they asked if anyone in the room (there were about 60 HR professionals in attendance) had jobs they were looking to fill. Several raised their hands and said they had jobs open, and two of them caught my attention: one was for an entry-level HR analyst, and the other was for an HR intern.

It just so happens that days before this luncheon, a young man with whom I have been acquainted for many years approached me about helping him find work in the HR area. He had just graduated from college with a Bachelor's degree in Communications, but was thinking he'd really like to work in HR.

With my friend James in mind, as soon as the meeting was over, I made a bee-line to both of those HR professionals and chatted with them about their jobs. I told them of my young friend, and extolled his qualities. They both expressed interest in seeing his resume. This afternoon, I sent the following e-mail message on James's behalf to both of the HR professionals who had openings:

> Maria,
> It was nice meeting you yesterday at the SHRM luncheon. Good information was provided, I thought.
>
> I am the one who spoke with you after lunch about the young man I am working with to help him find an entry-level HR position. His name is

James _____, and he's a great young man. I have probably known him since he was five years' old or thereabouts!

Anyway, I have attached his resume. He graduated in July and is excited about beginning a new chapter of his life – ie —> a real job! As you'll see from his resume, he has a Bachelor's of Science in Communications, and he has had a variety of work experiences in the business world.

I appreciate your willingness to take a look at him – you won't be sorry. As I mentioned yesterday – he will not be an HR problem for you. He has a great work ethic, good interpersonal skills and would be a delight to have in the office. And, while it's probably too early to tell, I suspect he has the instincts and intuition that makes good HR professionals. As an HR professional, I know you know that not everyone has those skills, and they cannot be taught.

May I have James contact you, or would you prefer to wait until you have weighed his resume and background against those of other candidates?

Daniel Quillen
Director of Internal Services
City of Aurora

If you can find someone who is willing to provide this type of introduction, you will increase your possibility of success many times over. While he has had some business experience ("…he has had a variety of work experiences in the business world."), none of it was directly related to HR. But with any luck, this introduction will open doors for him that may lead to employment.

So work with your network – get the word out that you're looking for work. Don't be afraid to tell them your predicament – great grades but no formal experience. Enlist their assistance and you may be able to end your search quickly.

Be creative

When I graduated from high school, one of the industries in which young people could make a lot of money quickly was construction. After applying at a number of construction companies and being rejected because of my lack of experience, I hit on a strategy that netted me a job which I worked off and on for several years, in between school semesters during the summer and even during Christmas and Spring breaks.

After introducing myself to the owner of a small steel construction company, I said something like:

> I do not have much construction experience. However, I have a strong work ethic, have good dexterity (I was a high school athlete), and can learn any-thing quickly. I will work for half wages until you feel I have gained enough experience for you to pay me full wages.

The company owner smiled and said something like: "Well, how can I beat that?! You start on Monday morning." Two weeks later when I received my first paycheck, I was gratified to see that he didn't hold me to my offer to work for half wages – he paid me a full wage.

Remember my fictional / composite recent graduate friend from Chapter 7, Auri-anna St. Pierre? Let's pretend (that's easy, since she's fictional…) that Ms. St. Pierre is in the situation we have been describing in this chapter – she focused on her grades to the exclusion of all else – and has zero formal experience in the business world. Her resume might look something like this:

AURIANNA ST. PIERRE

www.LinkedIn.com/in/astpierre   720-555-1212   astpierre@email.com

PROFESSIONAL SUMMARY

Rising business professional with exceptional attention to detail, passion and the drive to succeed. Strong, creative team player looking to make a contribution to the bottom line. Fluency in multiple languages (English, Spanish and German, with a smattering of Italian) provides an additional dimension that allows great flexibility. Strengths include:

• Driven to succeed	• Compensation	• Creativity
• Team Player	• Problem Solver	• Customer Service
• Self Starter	• MS Office	• Strong work ethic

EDUCATION

Bachelor of Science, Business Administration with Human Resources specialization, 3.8 GPA, magna cum laude

Brigham Young University, Provo, Utah

LEADERSHIP SKILLS AND ACCOMPLISHMENTS

Volunteer Server   **2004 to 2011**
Denver Rescue Mission

> • Volunteer server at rescue mission, providing hot meals and a warm smile to homeless individuals on weekends and holidays. Averaged 25 days of volunteer service per year between 2004 and 2011.

> • Selected to lead other volunteers in providing services. Many volunteers were older and had more years' experience.

> • Proposed ways to more efficiently feed over 200 people each meal. Changes resulted in less wasted food, and 20% quicker service to guests.

Explorer Scout   **2008 to 2010**
Boy Scouts of America

> • Participated in ride-alongs with Police officers of the City of Aurora, Colorado to learn the day-to-day duties of Police officers.

• Selected to lead team of citizen volunteers assisting in fingerprinting individuals at the city.

• Assisted Fire Department personnel in inspecting baby car seats and in providing annual "Bike Rodeo" designed to teach young children bicycle and street safety.

Gold Award Recipient   **2006 to 2009**
Girls Scouts of the USA

• (The Gold Award is the Girl Scout equivalent to the Eagle rank in Boy Scouts.)

• Completed 30 hours of leadership training and demonstration.

• Completed over 50 hours of career exploration; careers researched and investigated included Human Resources, Finance and Banking, Non-profit, City government, Public Safety (Police and Fire), and software development.

• Developed and implemented a community service project to provide toiletries and other personal items to women's shelters. Required to lead other Girl Scouts, leaders and community members in the project, which totaled more than 100 person-hours.

AWARDS AND HONORS

• Selected as Girl Scout troop representative to National Girl Scout Conference.

• Winner of several academic scholarships and one scholarship for exemplary volunteerism.

• Named Volunteer of the month three times by the Denver Rescue Mission and once by the City of Aurora, Colorado.

• National Spelling Bee representative from the State of Colorado, 2007

• Graduated magna cum laude with 3.8 GPA.

As you can see, in this instance our fictional friend has no real-world business experience, but she has been busy with community work. Better to share that information than none at all. The picture you get of Aurianna is that of an individual who cares about others, who succeeds in whatever she puts her hand to, and who is passionate about helping others.

What picture can you paint of yourself?

By the way – you'll note in this instance, **Aurianna led with her education**. As I mentioned in the previous chapter I normally do not recommend that unless you attended one of the top US schools. However, in Aurianna's lack-of-experience case, her education and GPA are perhaps her strongest elements – no sense burying them at the end of the resume.

As a reminder, please review Chapter 7 in its entirety for the basics of structuring your resume and leading with your strengths.

Your Resume / No Experience checklist

_____ I may have more experience than I think I have! Evaluate any extracurricular activities in which I have participated for the lessons I learned through them.

_____ Even though I have graduated, I should consider getting an internship to pick up much-needed experience.

_____ Networking may be one of the best tools for me as a graduate with no experience. Who do I know that can put a good word in for me, who can serve as an advocate for me?

_____ Be creative!

_____ Accentuate the positive, even though it may not be formally job related.

Cover Letters

When I go through hundreds of applications from people who all have very similar-sounding experience, cover letters are the only glimpse I have into a person's personality.
– Sophia Amoruso

One of the big questions in the job search world is whether or not you should write a cover letter to accompany your resume. Some hiring managers like them, in fact, prefer them, while others don't even look at them. As a hiring manager, I generally prefer looking at the resume, and often don't get to the cover letter, although I typically read the cover letter for the top candidates. But some of my peers do just the opposite. They scan the cover letter first, and if it piques their interest, they review the accompanying resume.

If in fact some hiring managers don't even look at cover letters, **why should you take the time to write one, much less tailor it for every position**? Let me answer that with a short story:

A few years ago I was screening resumes of recently graduated / bar-passed attorneys for my law firm. I had identified a half dozen top candidates and brought their resumes to our legal recruiting manager. All but one of the resumes had cover letters. As I handed her the stack of resumes and cover letters, I mentioned that one of them didn't have a cover letter. She said, "Well, if they don't care enough about the job to write a cover letter, then I am not interested in reviewing their resume." And she didn't. And that candidate missed out on a position with a starting salary of $120,000, all because the candidate didn't take the time to write a one-page cover letter.

Not knowing whether the HR department or hiring manager reviews cover letters, do you want to risk losing out on a job for the sake of a one-page letter that would probably take you five minutes to tailor? With my apologies to the writer of the poem *For Want of a Nail*:

FOR WANT OF A COVER LETTER
For want of a cover letter the interview was lost.
For want of an interview, the job was lost.
For want of a job the house was lost.
All for the want of a cover letter.

So, now that you've decided to write a cover letter….

Your cover letter should be as crisp and clean as your resume. There should be no typos. It should be short – absolutely no more than one page. Length in a cover letter is deadly. As with resumes, you have only a few moments to grab a reviewer's interest.

Like your resume, your cover letter should be tailored to every position for which you apply. Tailoring your cover letter isn't as extensive a process as the process for tailoring your resume, but it should still be attended to with care.

Let's look at a cover letter my fictional friend Aurianna from the previous two chapterss might write to accompany her resume:

August 22, 2015

Dear Hiring Manager,

I am responding to your job posting for the entry-level HR Analyst position listed on Indeed.com and your company's website. I have recently graduated from Brigham Young University with a Bachelor of Science degree in Business Administration with a specialty in Human Resources. In addition to my degree, I have a little over a year of HR experience. Between my degree and my HR work experience, I have knowledge and / or experience in most of the areas your job ad lists for the HR Analyst. Without going into exhaustive detail, following are a few of the specifics about my schooling and experience as they pertain to this position:

Legal compliance – while working as an HR intern, I had the opportunity of investigating employee complaints, including sexual harassment, hostile workplace, and requests for ADA (Americans with Disabilities Act) accommodations. I was able to successfully resolve all issues without legal action directed toward my company.

Employee Relations – part of my responsibility as an HR intern and again as an HR manager was to investigate employee complaints and attempt to resolve each of those complaints to the satisfaction of the complaining party. I was able to do this, and earned praise from my mentor and company management for the way I was able to handle each situation.

Benefits design – while I have no formal training in this area, I took several upper-level HR courses in benefits design and implementation, and was able to assist one company during my HR internship with the operational aspects of implementing a change in benefits – helping draft employee communications, manning an information booth at several open enrollment fairs, and assisting with crafting the presentation for employee meetings.

New-hire onboarding – one of my primary responsibilities while working as an HR intern was to learn and then take the lead on providing onboarding for new hires. My mentoring HR manager told me I was able to learn and then lead the onboarding process more quickly than any previous interns they have had at the company. I frequently received compliments from newly hired employees. In addition, I made several recommendations for ways to streamline the training, which were accepted and became part of the going-forward onboarding process.

*Recruiting and posting job ad*s – I was responsible for drafting and posting job ads, screening resumes and presenting the resumes for the top candidates to hiring managers. Hiring managers repeatedly commented on the quality of the candidates I was sharing with them.

Minimum qualifications -- In addition to my one year+ Human Resources experience, I have the passion and drive to strive for excellence in this position. As mentioned earlier, I also have a Bachelor's degree in business with a specialization in Human Resources.

I would be pleased to visit with you regarding this position to see how my skills and experience might help Acme Manufacturing exceed its strategic business initiatives and objectives. I can be reached at 303-555-1212 or astpierre@e-mail.com.

Thank you for your consideration,
Aurianna St. Pierre

Note – even though this cover letter covers several pages in this book, written in Times New Roman and with 12-point font, it fits nicely onto one 8½" x 11" page.

Let's discuss each of the sections of Aurianna's cover letter:

Date

August 22, 2015

As with all letters, you should date your cover letter. As you tailor your cover letters, this is one area you will want to be particularly vigilant in – if you use a cover letter template, don't forget to change the date of each or your letters. Speaking from experience, this is easy to overlook.

Salutation

> Dear Hiring Manager,

Whether you use *Dear Hiring Manager, Hiring Manager, Dear Recruiter, Human Resources Department* or some other salutation, you should have some sort of salutation in your letter. The very best thing is if you can find the name of the actual hiring manager, and address the letter directly to her or him. I would avoid using generic salutations such as *To Whom It May Concern* and *Dear Sir*.

If you do have the name of the hiring manager, make certain you spell that name correctly. Also, is Chris Jones a man or a woman? Unless you know for certain, don't guess – if you're wrong it's bad. Consider using:

> Dear Chris Jones,

If you know the hiring manager is a woman, do not use Miss or Mrs. in your salutation. Ms. is more than acceptable these days. If you are uncomfortable with that, then stay with *Dear Cynthia Jones* (and unless you know for sure, don't assume that Cynthia goes by Cindy).

Avoid addressing the hiring manager in a cover letter by their first name. While a generalization, this seems to be a tendency of many Millennials. Don't assume informality – a more formal greeting in your letter, as well as in person, is far more likely to impress than not. And besides, if you know the hiring manager's name is William, does he go by William, Will, Willie, Bill, Liam, or something else? Since I am one of many that goes by his middle name, I am always amused by people who assume informality with me and call me Bill (my first name is William). I suppose they are trying to establish a connection or rapport, but that's the wrong way to do that with me (and many others, I might add).

Should you use a comma or a colon? I prefer a comma, even though it is a business letter and a little more informal, but either will suffice. Do not confuse a colon (:) with a semi-colon (;) – they are not just different manifestations of the same punctuation mark. They have different uses, and if you are unsure which to use, find another punctuation mark!

Don't be too informal

Opening Paragraph

> I am responding to your job posting for the entry-level HR Analyst position listed on Indeed.com and your company's website. I have recently graduated from Brigham Young University with a Bachelor of Science degree in Business Administration with a specialty in Human Resources. In addition to my degree, I have a little over a year of HR experience. Between my degree and my HR work experience, I have knowledge and / or experience in most of the areas your job ad lists for the HR Analyst. Without going into exhaustive detail, following are a few of the specifics about my schooling and experience as they pertain to this position:

This is a quick snapshot of who you are. As a hiring manager, I am always interested in which advertising source candidates found my job listing. This is especially important if you learned of this position through a friend or family member who works for that company – you want their name to be front and center.

Be sure and mention the title of the position for which you are applying, and if there is a job number associated with it, include that.

> I am responding to the posting on the CareerBuilder website for an entry-level *Human Resources Analyst* (65796612) in Englewood, Colorado (reference ID 65805341_276281623).

Large companies in particular may have many positions listed simultaneously. If your cover letter says, "I am applying for the position I read about on your website," that's an invitation for your applications packet to find its way into the trash can. Busy HR departments and hiring managers don't have time to try and figure out which position you are interested in. Don't make it difficult on them.

As you open your cover letter, introduce your professional self by sharing your degree and the university from which you graduated. If you have any relevant work experience, the first paragraph is a good place to mention that as well. This begins to establish you as a credible candidate. If you have experience that relates to the job for which you are applying, this helps identify you as a qualified candidate for the position. If you are a barista or waitress, but are seeking a position as an interior designer, don't include your current position. Instead, open with something like: "I am seeking an opportunity to use my degree in interior design to further the success of Acme Interior Design Studios."

At the end of the first paragraph are the following two sentences:

> Between my degree and my HR work experience, I have knowledge and / or experience in most of the areas your job ad lists for the HR Analyst. Without going into exhaustive detail, following are a few of the specifics about my schooling and experience as they pertain to this position:

In her opening paragraph, Aurianna informed the hiring manager that she had recently graduated from college with a degree in Business and a specialization in Human Resources. She also let the hiring manager know that her HR knowledge came from two sources: classwork she had done and relevant work experience. Then she prepares them for the next section of her cover letter – she tells them she has experience in most of the areas they are seeking (she can only say that if it's true... she will have to modify that if not), *and she will share her experience as it relates to the position they posted*. She tailored her resume to the position for which she was applying, and she will also want to tailor her cover letter so it highlight the aspects of your education and any experience she has that specifically address those things identified in the job ad as being important to the hiring manager.

If your experience is limited to the coursework you have taken *and* is relevant to the particular position for which you are applying, then that's okay.

Remember during Chapter 7 we talked about the need to print out the job description and circle the key elements of the job? You used that exercise to identify the nine bullet points that would go in your *Professional Summary* section. Those same elements are important for your cover letter also. Except in your cover letter, you probably won't have the space to do more than four of five of them, so pick the four or five you feel are the most crucial for this position.

You might ask if it's okay to use the same elements in both your resume as well as your cover letter. My answer is "Yes!" Remember – we mentioned some hiring managers only read cover letters and others only read resumes. Some read both. Let's not overlook members of the hiring manager population who may only read one or the other document.

As in her resume, each of the skills and experience areas Aurianna lists has accomplishments associated with it. This is equally important in both cover letter and resume.

Remember – you are trying to convince some faceless person on the other end of the job search line that you have what it takes to help their company succeed. What better way than to outline the skills and experiences they are seeking and show how you have excelled in each of those areas? As we discussed, your experience may be limited to a three-month internship and coursework. If that's the case, then highlight that, and look for accomplishments in even those limited engagements.

Minimum Qualifications

In addition to my one year+ Human Resources experience, I have the passion and drive to strive for excellence in this position. As mentioned earlier,

I also have a Bachelor's degree in business with a specialization in Human Resources.

Most positions today have a *Minimum Qualifications* section to their job ad which clearly outlines the company's expectations regarding education, experience, licenses, certifications, etc. This sentence allows you to address how you stack up against those requirements. If you don't meet their minimum requirements in one (or more) of the areas, I wouldn't highlight it here.

Often, you'll see *Minimum Requirements* listed with a certain level of education (typically Bachelor's degree required, Master's degree preferred), or *relevant work experience*. That last little tag line allows the company some wiggle room to hire someone without a degree, and often cracks the door open a bit for candidates who have tremendous experience but no formal degree, or who they like and feel will be a fit for their company.

Remember – you'll have the most success in applying for jobs if you apply for positions that are entry level. Hiring managers know you won't have gobs of experience – perhaps only a short internship and/or coursework. So when you are applying for those positions, be sure and include whatever experience and coursework you have that is relevant to the position.

Closing Paragraph

I would be pleased to visit with you regarding this position to see how my skills and experience might help Acme Manufacturing exceed its strategic business initiatives and objectives. I can be reached at 303-555-1212 or astpierre@e-mail.com.

Remember, when you are applying for a job, it's not all about YOU, but all about what the hiring manager wants and needs. You just need to convince her or him that you are who they need to solve their problems.

In the past I have received advice that you should put a date that you'll be following up: "I'll call you next Tuesday to follow up on my resume to see if you have any questions." I am not a big fan of that. In fact, it's a little off-putting to me. It seems a little too forward and aggressive. I must admit, however, that some good friends of mine – seasoned professionals – have had great success with this approach and are comfortable using it. So the decision is up to you. But – if you say you are going to follow up next Tuesday (or Wednesday, Thursday, etc.) be sure you do!

Always list your contact number and your e-mail address.

Closing

> Thank you for your consideration,

I think anything here that is respectful is fine. Respectfully, Regards, Sincerely or the like are all fine.

Once again, I would avoid being too informal:

> Thanks!

I prefer *Thank you for your consideration* over *Thanks for your consideration*. I don't think it is a big deal, but I would go with the former.

Cover Letter Template

You may recall from Chapter 7 one of the tools I use is a resume template to tailor my resume and make that process more streamlined. This template has all the key components of my resume, along with thirty-five bullet points of my experiences and accomplishments. By taking the time to write each of these and place them in a template, they are available to cut and paste and insert into my tailored resume, already having been scrubbed for content, grammar, typos and accomplishments.

Likewise, I developed a cover letter template, filled with insertions that can be used to tailor my cover letter for any position for which I am applying. While my cover letter is one page, my cover letter template is six pages. And while the average cover letter may have four or five job experiences listed, my template has over fifty items. Each of these items was written in response to a job ad that called for expertise in one of these areas.

So let's consider some of the entries that might have been in our fictional friend Aurianna's cover letter template:

> *ADA compliance* – Investigated employee complaints, including sexual harassment, hostile workplace, Americans with Disabilities Act (ADA) accommodations; all complaints resolved without legal action.

> *Creativity* – Recommended the company begin a client newsletter to attract return visits from clients; company owners estimated newsletter was responsible for 23% increase in business over a six-month period ($50,000 to $75,000 increase in sales).

> *Federal employment laws* – Updated employee handbook, adding updated chapters on Fair Labor Standards Act (FLSA), ADA and Family Medical Leave Act (FMLA).

Note that each of Aurianna's entries begins with the category of the entry: *ADA compliance, Creativity, Federal employment laws*. Aurianna should list all these items alphabetically in her **cover letter template** for ease of location, *but in her cover letter, she should lead with the elements that seem most critical to the hiring manager of the position for which she is applying* (that is – they should not be listed alphabetically in her cover letter).

Sometimes you will want to have similar / duplicate entries in your cover letter template, to allow you to use similar entries for different company requirements. You may recall in the Chapter 7 I strongly encouraged you to use the hiring company's language. If their job ad called it *Recruiting*, you should use the term *Recruiting* in your cover letter. If they used *Talent Acquisition*, then that's the term you should use.

E-mail vs Attachment

I have had discussions with a number of Directors of HR and other hiring managers about whether or not they like cover letters to be attachments to an e-mail, or whether they prefer them to be embedded in the e-mail itself. I spoke with many such managers, and the resounding answer was: "It doesn't matter."

The fact of the matter is, however, that depending on the industry, most cover letters and resumes will end up as attachments or cut-and-paste posts in application software. More on that in the *Gatekeepers* chapter later in this book.

Cover Letters checklist

Be sure to write a cover letter!

_____ I should always write a cover letter.

_____ Make certain my cover letters are professional – no typos or grammar difficulties.

_____ Just like with my resume, I need to tailor every cover letter to every job.

_____ Highlight my skills and experience that are relevant to the job – even if that experience is only a short internship or coursework.

_____ As with my resume, add accomplishments to my cover letter.

_____ Do not be too informal in my cover letter salutation or at the end of the cover letter.

_____ Developing a cover letter template will help me as I tailor my cover letters to each job.

Network, Network, Network!

It's all about people. It's about networking and being nice to people and not burning any bridges. Your book is going to impress, but in the end it is people that are going to hire you.
– Mike Davidson

In 2001, I was working with Avaya, a spin-off from AT&T. To my amazement, Avaya offered an early retirement package that was too good to pass up, so I prepared to take the leap.

A week or so later, I was speaking with a group of friends at church. I indicated I would be leaving Avaya in about three weeks, and was looking for work as a Human Resource professional.

A week later I received a call from one of the men with whom I had been speaking:

Troy: "Dan, didn't you say you were looking for a job?"

Me: "Absolutely."

Troy: "And what did you say you did?"

Me: "I do Human Resources."

Troy: "That's what I thought. The Director of Human Resources at my law firm just announced he was leaving. Are you interested?"

Me: "Yes indeed. I would love to work for your firm, and I have the experience to do that job."

He agreed to contact the hiring manager about me and see if she would accept my resume. A day or two later he called back to say she would accept my resume.

I interviewed a few days later and was offered the job. The job offer was extended a few days prior to my early retirement from Avaya. I was leaving Avaya on a Wednesday. I could have started at the firm on Thursday, but decided I wanted to be retired for a while, so set my start date on the Monday following my retirement.

After I started with the firm, I asked the hiring manager why she had hired me. She said, "Well, your resume was a good one, and you had good experience. But had Troy not recommended you, I would not have invited you in for an interview because you had no law firm experience. But we trust Troy, and his recommendation swayed us to decide to interview you."

And with that, I began a wonderful ten-year career with a large law firm – all because a member of my network remembered I was looking for a job and put in a good word for me.

And that, my recently graduated friend, is what networking is about. Or – more precisely, that is what networking can be about. Let's dissect some of those paragraphs with which I opened this chapter:

> **1. I was looking for a job**. In my case, I took an early retirement package and was looking for another job. In your case, you are retiring as a full-time student and you're looking for a job.

> **2. I mentioned to a group of friends** in my social circle (this one happened to be church friends) **that I was looking for work**. Note that I didn't grill them or even ask them to find me a job.

3. My friend Troy, with my recent conversation still in his memory, called me when a position came open at his law firm, and he **remembered I was looking for work in that area**.

4. My friend was willing to put in a good word for me at his firm.

5. Had my friend not recommended me as a candidate, **I would not have had an interview** (and of course – wouldn't have gotten the job at which I worked for the next decade!)

6. Finally, I got the interview because the hiring manager trusted my friend and thought it was worth the risk.

I might add also that this wonderful job was never listed on any job boards or with any recruiter. The recruiting strategy for the firm was to just quietly reach out to individuals they knew in the industry and see if any of them were interested. Without networking, I would never have heard about this opportunity.

So…how do you, as a recent grad, go about networking?

Many jobs are never posted. Networking unlocks those jobs!

Here's what I recommend: Identify all your friends and acquaintances who might be in a position to know of jobs that might be available. Let them know you are looking for a job. and be sure they know your skills and experience.

Ten years after networking earned me that job, our law firm merge with another and I lost my job. Remembering the success I had a decade earlier, I turned to my network for assistance again. In addition to my LinkedIn network, I went through the address book in my e-mail and Facebook, and identified another 200 individuals: friends, neighbors, former work acquaintances (including a number at my former firm), fellow church members, vendors who had called on me, etc. I developed an e-mail list with all their e-mail addresses, then I sent them the following e-mail:

NETWORK, NETWORK, NETWORK!

Subject: A little assistance please!

Greetings,

As some of you may know, the law firm I have been at for the past decade has outsourced my role, so I am actively seeking a position at another firm or company. You are receiving this e-mail because you are someone I know and trust, and I am hoping you will assist me. As you know, most positions in today's work environment are gotten through networking. It occurred to me that all of you know far more people and have many more contacts in companies than I could ever possibly have, and that's where I need your assistance.

Periodically, I will send you a list of companies to which I have applied. Applying to companies today is generally through a faceless website that then scrubs your resume for key words. If you have the right key words, and the right number of them, your resume is forwarded to the hiring manager. If you do not have the specific key words, even though you may be the best qualified applicant, your resume may never be forwarded to a hiring manager.

And that's where you come in. If you know someone at one of the companies at which I have applied, a kind word to your contact on my behalf might enable my resume to reach them -- or they might be willing to call my resume to the attention of the hiring manager. Or -- even though they have my resume, it may be in a stack of 100s of resumes. Your support might be just the motivation for the hiring manager to seek and review my resume, especially if you attach my resume for them to review (I have attached my resume for your review and forwarding if you feel it appropriate).

I promise future e-mails will be much shorter, consisting mainly of the list of companies to which I have recently applied.

While you have my resume, let me share a few highlights:

• I am seeking a senior HR position (Director or VP)

• I have 20 years of progressively more responsible HR experience

• I have an MBA

• I am SPHR certified (sort of like a CPA designation for accountants)

If you have questions, please ask away. You may contact me at wdanielquillen@gmail.com or 303-555-1212.

Thanks for your assistance and consideration!

Daniel Quillen

After I sent the e-mail, responses were immediate from many of those to whom I sent the e-mail. I received many well wishes, and more than a few job leads from that initial e-mail. What's more, I now had 450 people in the business world keeping their eyes open for positions that might be appropriate for me.

Don't underestimate my network – use it!

A recruiter friend of mine feels so strongly about how effective networking can be that he tells his candidates: "Your net*work* is your net *worth*."

Then, as indicated in my e-mail to my network of friends, every week to ten days I sent an e-mail that went something like this:

Subject: Dan Quillen job search update

Greetings Friends,

NETWORK, NETWORK, NETWORK!

As indicated in my earlier e-mail, I am following up to let you know the job search activities I have been pursuing. I have submitted resumes to the following companies:

- Acme manufacturing
- Arrow Electronics
- Ball Industries
- Cisco
- Comcast
- Eureka Company
- Leprino Foods
- Newmont Mining
- Western Union

And I have gotten interviews at the following companies with the following individuals:

- Leprino Foods – Angie Jones (internal recruiter, I think)
- Newmont Mining – Mary Jones (internal recruiter; hiring manager is Dan Smith)
- Western Union – Cindy Thompson, VP of HR

If you have contacts at any of these companies (either the ones I have applied to or the ones I have interviews with), I would appreciate if you could put a good word in for me.

I will keep you all updated on the progress and whether any of these interviews yields positive results.

Thanks for your assistance!

Dan Quillen

Once again, I heard from many folks in my network – some said they didn't know anyone at those companies, but were keeping me in their prayers / sending positive thoughts my way. Some responded with information about jobs available in their company, others offered to reach out to the person with whom I was interviewing.

All in all – it was a very positive and motivating experience for me.

Networking – Groups

As I mentioned in an earlier chapter, there are many networking groups out there that may be of assistance to you in your job search. Some of them are industry specific, others are governmental groups (for example, the county I live in has networking groups for people seeking work), churches often have networking groups for members of their church (and other denominations as well). Check them out – they may be a great job search tool for you.

One of the most helpful groups I was a member of was offered by my church. As detailed earlier in this book, on the first Tuesday of each month, members of my church met at a local Mexican food restaurant and held a networking meeting. It was a great group – employers and job seekers all together, breaking bread and sharing needs ("I need an IT professional…" and "I am looking for an HR opportunity…"). Very positive.

Networking works both ways…

For networking to truly work for you, you need to understand it works both ways. Today you are searching for work, and tomorrow you'll be employed because you had someone care enough to take the time and provide an introduction, or who hand-carried your resume to the hiring manager and provided a good word in your behalf. When I got the job I currently have, the wife of one of the top executives at the organization put a good word in for me. She and I had worked together at the law firm I have mentioned several times in this book. She told her husband to tell the hiring manager that: "He would be crazy if he doesn't hire Dan." How's that for a wonderful reference?!

NETWORK, NETWORK, NETWORK!

You will one day be in the place where you have the opportunity to return grace for grace – by bringing a job to the attention of a job searcher, or put a good word in for her, carry her resume to the hiring manager, etc. Look for opportunities to return the favor.

And – be sure and use social networking as much as you can!

Network, Network, Network! checklist

_____ Using my network of friends and acquaintances is a power tool in my job search.

_____ Many jobs are never posted on job boards. Networking unlocks those jobs!

_____ Send an e-mail to all my acquaintances, letting them know I have graduated and am now looking for work.

_____ Every week to ten days, send an update to my network about my job search – companies where I have applied, interviews I have scheduled, etc.

_____ Give back to my network; work for others who contact me during their job hunt like I hope people will help me!

_____ My network is my net worth!

Social Networking

Instead of telling the world what you're eating for breakfast, you can use social networking to do something that's meaningful. – Edward Norton

I am certain there's not much this Baby Boomer author can tell you, a Millennial, about social networking. In fact, you could probably sit down and write a LOT more about that social marvel than I can. However, what you might not be aware of is that social media is a great way to search for work – and a very important arrow in your job search quiver.

That great source of all knowledge, Wikipedia, defines Social Networking as:

> Social media refers to the means of interactions among people in which they create, share, and/or exchange information and ideas in virtual communities and networks....Furthermore, social media depends on mobile and web-based technologies to create highly interactive platforms through which individuals and communities share, co-create, discuss, and modify user-generated content. It introduces substantial and pervasive changes to communication between organizations, communities, and individuals....

> In today's economy, job hunters need to use every tool available to them in their job hunt, and that includes social networking.

So – see – I am not the only one telling you that you need to use social networking for your job search!

While there are many tools to assist you in your social networking, the three primary ones today are LinkedIn, Facebook and Twitter. Each deserves a few moments' consideration as tools to assist you in your job search. I'll address each one in order, based on their usefulness in networking. From a usefulness perspective, I prioritize them as:

1. LinkedIn
2. Facebook
3. Twitter

LinkedIn

LinkedIn (www.linkedin.com) is a massive organization topping 200 million participants, many of whom may be able to assist you in finding work (it's just finding the right one!). In addition to being a place where you can have an online resume / presence, you can also connect to friends, colleagues, customers, etc. Those connections, and individuals connected to them may provide opportunities for you to bring an end to your employment search.

Once you set up a LinkedIn account, you go about identifying people you want to include in your network. Use the *Search* box on the homepage to do this. The *Search* box has a drop-down box that provides several search options, including *People, Companies* and *Jobs*. You can search for people by their name, or you can search for them by company.

Once you identify individuals with whom you would like to connect, simply click on their name, and you'll be able to click a *Connect* button, which will send a message to them, asking them to connect to you. Then, all they have to do is accept your invitation, and voila! you are connected.

When you have a few connections, LinkedIn, smart application that it is, will share with you *People You May Know* – people that are connected to the people you know. So if you connected with people from a former employer, all the sudden your *People You May Know* section will be filled with other people from that same company (because they are connected to some of the people you just connected with). Other people your connections know will also be displayed. To connect with those you know, simply click on the *Connect* button, voila! – you have more people in your network!

Once you are a member of LinkedIn (there is no cost to join the basic level), you can search companies in which you are interested to see if you have any connections at those companies. If you do, you can reach out to them to let them know you are interested in a job at their company, and perhaps you can get an introduction to the hiring manager, or perhaps they will agree to carry your resume to the hiring manager with a good word.

So – let me show you how that might work. Let's say you are very excited – you submitted a resume to IBM for a position that would be a perfect match for you. About half an hour ago, an internal recruiter from IBM called you to tell you the hiring manager had reviewed your resume and would like to interview with you. Calmly, you say yes, that would be fine. You work with the recruiter and set a time and place for the interview.

As soon as you hang up, your first thought is: "Who do I know at IBM?" The answer is a little disconcerting – you know no one – or at least no one you are aware of. What to do?

Then you recall all the people with whom you are connected through LinkedIn. You go to the LinkedIn website and start poking around. From the navigation bar on your home page, you click on *Interests*. A drop-down box with three options appears:

- Companies
- Groups
- Influencers

You click on *Companies*, and you're taken to a page that has a *Search* box; you type in *IBM*, hoping that you find someone whom you know that works there. You click on the *Search* icon, and suddenly the pictures of five people appear. You recognize two of them immediately – one goes to church with you and the other was a former college roommate. Both of them are noted as 1st-degree connections – meaning you either accepted their invitation to connect, or they accepted your invitation. This is exciting – there are two people whom you know well who may be able to provide some positive input to the hiring manager with whom you are interviewing. You reach out to them (either via a message though LinkedIn, their personal e-mail address, or possibly even a phone call), explain about your upcoming interview, and see if one of them knows the hiring manager. Even if neither of them knows the hiring manager (IBM is a large company!), one or both of them may be willing to provide a positive reference to her / him.

Next, you turn your attention to the other three people, all listed as 2nd-degree connections. A 2nd-degree connection is connected to someone with whom you share a 1st-degree connection. None of these second-degree connections looks familiar. You click on the picture of the first one, and you see that he is connected to a woman with whom you worked a few years earlier. While this 2nd-degree connection doesn't know you, he does know your former coworker, and he might be willing to let the hiring manager know what a great guy your former colleague thinks you are. So you reach out to her, let her know what you need – a positive reference – and she agrees. You ask her to reach out to the fellow who is her 1st-degree contact (your 2nd-degree), and again, she agrees. Things are looking pretty good for you.

You check out the other two individuals listed as 2nd-degree connections, and the people they know that are connected to you aren't as close to you, and would probably not be able to provide much of a reference for you.

Even though you're excited about the interview with IBM, you know you need to keep searching for work. Back on your LinkedIn homepage, on the navigation bar, you see a tab for *Jobs*, and you select it. In the *Search* box that appears, you can type in a search string: *Human Resources Colorado, Medical sales, Phoenix,* etc. When the jobs come up, they will also tell you how many people in your network work at that company. Clicking on that notification lists all those individuals, and where they are in your network. It will let you know if any of your connections are connected to the hiring manager, which provides a great opportunity for you.

I want to share another very powerful way to use LinkedIn in your job search. When you first begin looking for work, **LinkedIn provides an awesome opportunity to get the word out that you are searching for work**, the kind of work you are seeking, and your qualifications to work in that field. To let your network know you are out of work:

From your LinkedIn homepage, there is a **text box** adjacent to your picture. (The text box will be next to your picture if you have posted a picture of yourself. If not – you should. Make certain it is a professional-looking picture.) You can place a message of up to 600 characters in that box. For example, here's a message a recent graduate might post:

> Greetings! I am reaching out to my LinkedIn network to tell you I am finally graduating! In May I graduate from the University of Southern California with a Bachelor's of Science in Electrical Engineering with specialization in robotics. I am looking for an opportunity to use my knowledge and the experience I gained during an internship in robotics at SCL Enterprises. I am excited to enter the industry and use my learning and experience with a top-notch company. I would prefer to stay in California, but am willing to go anyplace in the US. If you know of any such positions, please let me know!

Once you have entered your text in the box, select whether you want it to go to your LinkedIn network (it will go to your 1st-, 2nd- and 3rd-degree connections), LinkedIn + Twitter (remember -- only the first 140 characters will post to Twitter), or just to your 1st-degree Connections (select Connections).

To illustrate the power of LinkedIn: Had I posted the above announcement, I would have had many people who would have learned of my job search. As of this writing, I have 538 connections. As soon as I post a message, 538 of my closest friends will be notified that I have posted the message. AND all their connections – my 2nd-degree connections. AND all their connections (my 3rd-degree connections). I have no idea how many 1st-, 2nd-, and 3rd-degree connections I have, but it must number in the thousands, if not tens of thousands. I didn't want to go through all 538 of my connections to see how many 1st-degree connections they had (my 2nd-degree connections) – that would be too time-consuming. But I decided to take a sample: I looked at the first ten of my connections listed. Of those ten connections, there were 3,992 1st-degree connections, an average of 399 connections per person…sort of. Individuals with more than 500 connections only list "500+ connections" (and five of the ten connections I checked had more than 500 connections). So, I have at least 3,992 connections from those ten individuals. If all 538 of my connections average 399 1st-degree connections in their networks, then as soon as I post a message, 214,662 individuals receive notification of my message – and that's only my 1st- and 2nd- degree connections. Add the 3rd-degree connections, and the number is unimaginably large! That is part of the power of using LinkedIn in your job hunt!

Connect with LOTS of people through LinkedIn

As you explore LinkedIn, I think you'll quickly see how valuable and powerful it can be to assist you in your networking, and it will amaze you at how quickly your network will build with just a little effort on your part.

In addition to connections in LinkedIn, a valuable opportunity exists by joining groups aligned with the career field you have chosen. Sales, nursing, accounting, engineering, construction, legal, etc., and about any career you can imagine has a discussion group. Join them – they offer you the opportunity to meet and connect with other people in your potential profession / industry. Participate in the discussion groups – remember, though, that your responses are accessible to everyone in the group, so be circumspect in what you say. Have knowledge about a question or problem someone in the group has? Then offer your assistance. Weigh in. Have a good question that others might be able to answer? Then post it by all means. It was by participating in an industry discussion group that I learned of a number of job openings, and interviewed for one of them.

Of the three social networking sites covered in this chapter, LinkedIn gets my vote as the most valuable for networking while looking for a job.

Facebook

As mentioned earlier, I think LinkedIn far outperforms Facebook and Twitter as a job-hunting tool. But Facebook has its advantages, too. Consider your Facebook "friends" – here are potentially several hundred (or more) individuals – family members, colleagues, friends and acquaintances, who may be ready networkers for you. A word on Facebook about your search for employment and request for assistance may result in a lot of activity, including the possibility of obtaining work. In fact, I am aware of a number of friends who put the word out on Facebook and within a very short time they had found employment, based on the input and information from their friends.

Here's how it works on Facebook. Let's say I post essentially the same announcement I shared as an example in the LinkedIn section:

> Greetings! I am reaching out to my LinkedIn network to tell you I am finally graduating! In May I graduate from the University of Southern California with a Bachelor's of Science in Electrical Engineering with specialization in robotics. I am looking for an opportunity to use my knowledge and the experience I gained during an internship in robotics at SCL Enterprises. I am excited to enter the industry use my learning and experience with a top-notch company. I would prefer to stay in California, but am willing to go anyplace in the US. If you know if any such positions, please let me know!

Remember – LinkedIn is limited to 600 characters, so I had to be somewhat economical with my words there. But on Facebook, I know of no limit (other than people's willingness to read pages and pages of comments!), but you should probably keep your message somewhat short and sweet.

I have 400 friends on Facebook. The moment I post this above message, those 400 people see and will hopefully read about my job search. Also, with any luck, one or more of them will be aware of an open position – perhaps at their company, or at the company of a friend or neighbor, or any number of ways.

But you can also expand your Facebook network, similar to what was done in LinkedIn, although not quite as automatic or as dramatic. Once you post your comment ("What's on your mind?") on Facebook, ask all your friends to *Share* your post. If they will do that, it will exponentially multiply the number of people who are seeing your post and know you are looking for work – a good deal! However, it's not automatic as it is in LinkedIn, and my experience is that few Facebook friends – certainly nowhere near 100% -- will share your post. Some will, and perhaps many will, but not 100%.

As valuable a tool as Facebook is, there are dangers associated with it. Recruiters and hiring managers routinely check the Facebook accounts of individuals applying for jobs. If they see you doing or saying stupid things on Facebook, you may miss out on employment opportunities. If you must include your wild side to the world, do it through a pseudonym or stage name.

While I was writing this book, a Facebook employment *faux pas* went viral. A young woman in the Dallas-Fort Worth area – a single mother – announced to her Facebook friends that she had gotten a job in a daycare center. Along with her announcement, she posted an unfortunate message on Facebook:

> I start my new job today, but I absolutely hate working at daycares. Lol it's all good, I just really hate being around a lot of kids.

The Facebook world went nuts, and unfortunately one of those who heard about it was…you guessed it – her new boss, who called her to tell her not to bother reporting for work. She was fired before she even started.

And unfortunately, this isn't an isolated event. In recent years, press coverage has revealed other well-publicized incidents that resulted in people being fired because of things they posted on Facebook. In one case, it was information critical of the management of the person's company, and in another, an individual revealed information about a new product that was under development by his company. In both cases, the courts upheld the firings. So be warned, and be careful.

Twitter

Twitter is a social networking phenomenon that has risen in importance in recent years. It's a way of sharing short, quick bites of information – tweets – with friends and colleagues (tweeple). Since Twitter limits messages to 140 characters, you don't have to worry about people going on and on. Some might be tempted to dismiss Twitter

Be very careful on Facebook!

because of the brevity of the messaging. After all, how much important information can just a few characters provide?

If you are among those who question the value of short messages, consider the following:

- "I only regret that I have but one life to give for my country." Nathan Hale (74 characters)

- "Give me liberty or give me death." Patrick Henry (48 characters)

- "That's one small step for man, one giant leap for mankind," Neil Armstrong (74 characters)

- "Never was so much owed by so many to so few." Winston Churchill (62 characters)

As well as the following:

- "I am not a crook." Richard M. Nixon (35 characters)

- "I did not have sexual relations with that woman." William Jefferson Clinton (66 characters)

- "Read my lips – no new taxes." George H. W. Bush (47 characters)

- "A crude and disgusting video sparked outrage throughout the Muslim world." Barack Obama (95 characters)

So 140 characters can convey powerful messaging, for good or ill. Let's talk a little more about Twitter as a tool in your job search arsenal.

As with LinkedIn and Facebook, you have the opportunity to add many individuals – friends, colleagues, vendors, etc., to the network you can use for your job search. You can let your Lists (your Twitter network) know you are graduating, what kind of job you are seeking, or about an upcoming interview with a company.

Using the example I used in the LinkedIn and Facebook sections, if I sent the exact same message, it would be:

> Greetings! I am reaching out to my LinkedIn network to tell you I am finally graduating! In May I graduate from the University of Southern C

Hmmm – that's probably not the most efficient message to send via Twitter. It probably needs to be tweaked (tweeped?) quite a bit; something more like:

> Graduate in May w/ BSEE in robotics from USC! Had robotics internship & classes. Looking for entry-level robotics gig in Cal. Can you help?

Quite a different (written) message, although most of the critical points are included. (Information about where the internship was, how excited he is to work in robotics, etc., can be shared later.)

Let me provide a short contextual tutorial on Twitter vocabulary, since it's a little different than what you might be used to in Facebook and LinkedIn. Here you go:

English	Facebook	LinkedIn	Twitter
Message	Status Update	Status	Tweet
People in network	Friends	Connections	Lists
Someone you follow	Friends	Connections	Friend
Someone who follows you	Friends	Connections	Follower
Forwarding a message	Share	Share	Retweet
Private message	Message	Send a Message	Direct Message (DM)
Subject line:	–	–	hashtag (#)

That last item in the table may require a bit of explanation. Remember, Twitter limits users (tweeple) to 140 characters. A definite Twitter shorthand has evolved to allow tweeple to maximize those 140 characters. So instead of saying:

> Graduate in May w/ BSEE in robotics from USC! Had robotics internship & classes. Looking for entry-level robotics gig in Cal. Can you help?

Perhaps you say:

> #jobsearch - Grad nxt mnth w/ BSEE n robotics frm USC. Had robotics internship & classes. Lookng 4 entry-lvl rbtics gig in Cal – can u help?

Unfortunately that leaves no extra characters with which to wax eloquent (elqnt).

Seriously – the hashtag (pound sign to some of us – #) tells your followers the title of your topic.

SOCIAL NETWORKING

So why Twitter instead of Facebook and LinkedIn? Or in addition to? There are some fundamental differences between these three social networking platforms. We've mentioned the obvious: the 140-character limit on Twitter is pretty…limiting. Facebook has no maximum I have discovered (I have Friends that go on and on…and on), and LinkedIn has a 600-word limit.

Beyond that – in Facebook and LinkedIn, to follow someone, you must Friend them, or request a Connection. If the person you have made such a request to does not respond…you're not in their network and you cannot follow them (unless someone in your network is in their network and shares their comment). While Facebook and LinkedIn are private parties, Twitter is more like a Mosh Pit – all comers welcome and allowed! You do not have to be accepted by someone to follow them. Think about a famous personality who keeps her fans abreast of her latest activities – she doesn't have to accept 8,432,000 Friend requests – she can just send a tweet out, and all those who are following her will receive it. Or – in a job-search scenario – perhaps you follow several recruiters in your industry, or follow a number of companies who use Twitter to post positions (with Millennials in mind, probably). In recent years, more and more recruiters and companies are using Twitter to get the word out about jobs.

One of your job-search Twitter goals should be: Retweeting. As with Facebook and LinkedIn, Twitter users have their networks – lists. As you post information about your job search, you hope your list of followers will retweet (share) your tweet with their lists – thus multiplying the number of people who know about your job search and may be in a position to assist you.

As with Facebook and LinkedIn, individuals can respond to you – if you are a follower of the sender, then the process is a Direct Message (DM); if you are not a follower of the sender, they can still reach you by sending a public message (called @Reply). You'll get the message, but so will your list of tweeple.

One of the strengths of Twitter is its real-time aspects. LinkedIn and Facebook are somewhat real-time, but Twitter is as real-time as it gets. News about events world-wide are flashed over Twitter. That means you may be able to get the inside track on jobs that are posted – if you are on Twitter.

Recruiters and internal company recruiters are beginning to use Twitter more and more – they post jobs on Twitter to targeted groups of candidates. If you are not on Twitter, you may be left out and never even learn about the availability of jobs for which you are qualified.

As you can see, this social networking is more than just for social networking; perhaps it could be called *Employment* networking!

Definitely use social networking in my job search!

Social Networking checklist

_____ LinkedIn, Facebook and Twitter are strong networking and job search tools – use them!

_____ Learn how to get the most out of LinkedIn, Facebook and Twitter.

_____ Be careful what I post – recruiters, hiring managers and HR representatives often turn to social media to check out candidates. Don't do anything stupid!

Best Job-Search Sites for Recent Grads

Anyone who has never made a mistake has never tried anything new.
– Albert Einstein

I am often asked whether there are good websites for college students and recent grads to use in their quest for internships and employment, or should they just use the ones other job seekers use. My answer is – use both! Some of the large job boards – Monster.com, Indeed.com, etc. are for everyone to use, and they provide great assists for college students and recent graduates. But there are a number of other websites that are either focused on college students and recent graduates, or are very effective for them to use. Below is a Baker's Dozen (13) of the best job search websites for college students and recent graduates. They are not in prioritized order, but I have included a bit of information about each site.

AfterCollege.com – this is a highly regarded website that lists entry-level opportunities for college graduates. An element of AfterCollege.com is the ability to network with alumni from your school – individuals who, whether they know you or not – may be willing to provide help to a student from their former school. The power of alumni support should not be ignored nor understated. They may be able to provide that foot in the door you need to secure a job at their company.

AlumniCentral.com – this website uses the power of alumni relationships to provide a half million entry-level and other level jobs to job seekers. They also offer articles pertinent to job seekers, including career advice, resume and interviewing tips, etc. You'll be able to create your resume online and a profile on the website.

CareerRookie.com – Career Rookie is a website dedicated to students seeking internships and recent college grads seeking employment and have one thing in common – no experience. They post only internship and entry-level positions on their site. They have a blog as well, with a number of interesting articles and posts that are beneficial. Career Rookie is not as sophisticated as some of the other sites listed here, but worth the time and energy to learn how to use it.

CollegeRecruiter.com – this is a great website for internships and entry-level jobs. Like many of the websites focused on college students and recent graduates, it also offers articles and advice through its pages. It's certainly well worth a visit.

CollegeTopTalent.com – this is a unique job hunting site for college students and recent graduates, as stated in CollegeTopTalent's own words, here is their objective: *We are focused on students and recent graduates only. College Top Talent helps both young talents, who look for a job, and solid companies, who look for young talents to hire them for entry-level positions, find each other quickly: our dating-style model will match a graduate's appropriate skills with an employer's needs.* What's not to like about that? Students create their own profiles on the site, including their resume and "personal pitches." A 60-second video option is also available to job seekers. They also include career and job-searching advice on their website.

Craigslist.org – this is a career website that often gets overlooked or perhaps even disregarded by college students and grads, and yet it is a rich source of entry-level jobs. Not every company has the fancy websites that the 800-pound gorillas in the business world have, and yet these companies are looking for employees with your educational background and are willing to hire you even though you have no experience – that's a great deal. Often, these will be smaller or mid-size companies – companies that may prove to be a perfect stepping stone to opportunities at other, larger companies if that is your objective. So they use websites like Craigslist to list their entry-level positions. As I was writing this section, I went to Craigslist in Denver and was able to find hundreds of entry-level (i.e. – little or no experience required) positions. There were actually probably thousands of jobs.

BEST JOB-SEARCH SITES FOR RECENT GRADS

GrooveJob.com – this is a great job website for finding part-time and seasonal jobs for students – both those who are still in school as well as for recent graduates. It is one of the largest such websites out there. Like some of the other websites listed in this section, it provides various articles that may help you in your job search.

iHipo.com – this is a great website for students who are looking to work outside the boundaries of the United States. Their search boxes allow you to enter the kind of job you're looking for (engineering, geology, human resources, etc.) and the country you'd like to search. It's kind of an exciting website and if you are interested in working outside the USA, you should look into it.

Indeed.com – I have to include Indeed.com because I am a big fan of its aggregation capabilities – it has a lot of jobs pulled from many sources. It's not focused on students and recent graduates, and it's a little difficult from that standpoint, but it's definitely a website I recommend all graduates to use in their job search.

Jobing.com – this is another great website that is used by smaller and mid-size companies to post their entry-level positions. Larger companies also use this website, and it's certainly worth your time and energy checking it out.

USAJobs.gov – the USAJobs website has a section specifically focused on students and recent graduates interested in working in the federal government. Whether you wish to work as a public servant for your career, or just want to use such an opportunity as a springboard into the private sector after a few years, this is a good website to consider.

YouTern.com – Youtern is focused specifically on internships for college students, so may be of limited use to recent college graduates. However, if you spent your college career focusing on your studies and do not have any relevant experience to contribute when you are competing for a job, you may want to seek an internship even if you are in reality seeking a full-time job. It may be a way to gain some experience that will serve to make you a more attractive candidate to other companies.

Youtern has an award-winning blog that has some great and relevant posts for college students.

Alumni association websites – many universities have alumni association websites, and this is something you should avail yourself of. Many provide job opportunities (alums are encouraged to place jobs they have open or are aware of on the website), networking and career counseling for alumni.

Best Job Search Sites for Recent College Grads checklist

_____ These are all great websites for me to use as I look for work and internships.

_____ Don't discount government or non-profit jobs – they allow me to give back to the community while still earning a living.

_____ Don't overlook Craigslist for entry-level positions!

_____ Indeed.com is a great all-around website, an aggregator, which I should be sure and use in my job search.

Before the Interview

One important key to success is self-confidence. An important key to self-confidence is preparation. – Arthur Ashe

I have spent many hours in locker rooms before athletic contests. Taped ankles and wrists, stretching, icing, the guy in the corner by himself, concentrating on shutting out all the hub-bub and trying to mentally prepare for the upcoming contest. All are part of the pre-game preparation.

Before arriving in the locker room prior to the Big Game, more preparation occurred – drills on the most basic elements of the game – tackling drills, wind sprints, agility drills, running the bases, taking batting practice, "turning two," swimming laps, kick turns, practicing takedowns, reverses and holds.

All in preparation for the Big Game. And that's what you need to be about prior to your Big Game – The Interview.

Congratulations – you made the cut – not only are you on the varsity team, you're starting the game. You know you need to prove yourself. The spotlight is on you. Time to review your preparation, to psych yourself up to peak performance.

Networks

Earlier in the *Network, Network, Network!* chapter, we talked about identifying a network of individuals who could help you in your job search. Now that you've gotten an interview, use your network again.

Send a short note to your network, something along the lines of:

> All,
>
> Thanks for your work on my behalf these past few months. I have good news -- later this week I have an interview with Acme Company. The hiring manager with whom I will be meeting is Robert Smith.
>
> I would love to hear from anyone who knows Mr. Smith, Acme or anyone that works at Acme. Any insights, thoughts and / or putting in a good word on my behalf would be appreciated.
>
> Regards,
>
> Dan

Research

An important part of your job search comes when you have been contacted to come in for an interview. Immediately you should begin learning all you can about the company with which you will be interviewing.

Become extremely familiar with all aspects of this company. Go to their website and follow every link, read every scrap of information you can find, so that you learn all you can about the company. Read newspaper stories (easily obtained on the Internet), comments on investment websites, etc.

One of my favorite sources of information on companies is their **Annual Report**. All publically traded companies have annual reports, and most can be found online. These reports can be a gold mine of company information. They almost always have an introduction from the CEO or president of the company. They will often provide information about company strategies (e.g., expanding their European markets, focusing on the Pacific Northwest, etc.). Comments about recent mergers – or proposed mergers, recent acquisitions, divestitures, etc. are all good information to have in your back pocket as you head into your interview.

I have preached this principle many times in recent years to those with whom I have met to assist in their job searches, and I almost always follow that counsel myself. And yet, notwithstanding that, I went to a job interview after having scanned the company's website in a perfunctory manner. May I tell you my chagrin when the first question I was asked in the interview was: "What do you know about our company?" Here was an opportunity to shine by showing how informed I was about their company history, current markets, growth and strategy, etc. I failed miserably. My mind nearly went blank – because there was precious little in there about this company. I uttered a few thoughts, but even to me it sounded pretty lame. I kicked myself for the rest of the interview, and I daresay it negatively affected my performance during the rest of the time with the hiring manager. It was, to put it bluntly, an opportunity missed.

And I knew better! So don't find yourself in the same situation – prepare yourself. If you aren't asked, "What do you know about our company?" during the interview, you should find a way to work your knowledge in. For example, at the end of most interviews I have been on, I have been asked, "Do you have any questions for me?" This is your opportunity to show them you have an interest in the company beyond merely interviewing for a job. "Why yes, I do. In your most recent annual report I see where your CEO, Mr. Brown, said you were 'going full-speed ahead' into Europe. Will that move have any impact on the department I will be working in?"

Dress for Success

In the past decade or so, we have seen the business environment morph from extremely business-like and professional to more informal and relaxed. Because of that, you may be tempted to dress casually for your job interview. Please do not make this mistake; it is something you have 100% control over, and a "costume malfunction" could cost you that great job that is just perfect for you. I have always been a proponent of dressing well for job inter-

Research the companies I will interview with

views. By "dressing well" for professional jobs, I mean a dark suit (preferably dark blue or gray), white shirt and tie. Wing-tip shoes if you own them.

Let's briefly discuss each element of your dress:

Suit

Classic-cut suits are the best. First of all, you don't have to replace your suit every time fashions change. Remember leisure suits? (Have you ever heard of them? If not – no big loss…they were an unfortunate fashion trend in the mid-1970s.)

Dark suits are my preference – blue, blue pinstripe or gray – very conservative. I am not a fan of black because they feel…funeral-ish.

In the 1980s, it was fashionable for women to wear a white shirt, dark blue skirt and jacket, accentuated with a feminine red tie – the power colors. That is no longer necessary. Women no longer have to look like men when interviewing for a position. They do, however, need to dress professionally. As with men, dark colors are important, although women can get away with warmer colors like brown or green.

Shirt

I recommend either a white shirt or a very light blue shirt, but white is preferable. Your shirt and suit should be recently cleaned and pressed. When I first started my job hunt, a friend of mine gave me some of the best advice I received during my search: he told me to reserve my "interview suit," shirt and tie just for that purpose. Both your suit and shirt should be freshly cleaned. Your shirt should be starched – it only costs about $1.50 – after each wearing. I prefer heavy starch, but medium or light would do. I recall feeling like a million bucks when I "suited up" for an interview wearing my suit pants with the crisp crease and my gleaming starched white shirt.

Women's blouses should be conservative and certainly not provocative. Sheer, tight-fitting blouses have no place in the business world and especially not at a job interview. Nylons are essential for your job interview. I always appreciate women who come to job interviews dressed conservatively and professionally.

Tie

Add to your interview suit a conservative – not too skinny and not too wide – red or blue tie. It, too, should be freshly pressed, but you don't need to dry clean it after every interview unless it has gotten wrinkled or had something spilled on it. A serviceable tie can be purchased for under $25. (Need I say no ties with cartoon characters, holiday messages, political statements or beer product advertising should be worn?)

Belt

Don't forget a conservative business belt. Like your tie, it should be of conservative width (not too thin and not too wide), with a simple silver or gold clasp. It should match the color of your shoes, which should be black. You can pick up such a belt for $15 to $20 at Wal-Mart, Kohl's, Pennys, Sears, etc. As a recent graduate, you may be on a tight budget, so don't overlook Goodwill or other thrift stores. I have found some wonderful, nearly new leather dress belts for under $5.00.

For women, if your outfit needs or takes a belt, by all means accessorize. But the same rule applies to women as it does to men – belts should be conservative and not flashy or extreme.

Shoes

Your shoes don't have to be wingtips, but black, conservative shoes should be your goal. Dark suits and brown shoes don't go together. So be aware and conscious of that when you dress for success.

I will admit that the fashion circles out there today have declared brown shoes with navy and light or medium gray suits are acceptable. I still think they look funny, and oddly out of place, but you could probably get away with it.

Your shoes should be freshly polished to a high gleam.

Women should also wear conservative shoes. A pump or moderate heel is fine, but you shouldn't wear spike heels to your job interview. And ladies – don't forget to polish your shoes also. If you are short, you might consider a little higher heel; conversely, if you are already tall, you might go with lower heels or flats.

Are my shoes shined?

Socks

By now you've probably figured out that I recommend conservative socks with your suit. Now is not the time to make a statement. Even if it's Christmastime, please don't wear socks with reindeer and Santa on them.

Women should always wear nylons to job interviews.

Jewelry

The rule of thumb for successful interviewing is to go easy on the jewelry. If you have a heavy bracelet or watch that clunks on the table whenever you write, it would be best to leave that particular item of jewelry home. Women – your ear rings and necklaces should be conservative – dangling ear rings or heavy necklaces may draw attention away from the real message you are trying to get across.

Piercings – beyond ear rings – are another matter you'll have to decide for yourself, I am afraid. I think piercings are much more acceptable today than they were just a few years ago. However, many employers with customer-facing openings (sales, receptionists, etc.) are hesitant to hire those with significant piercings.

Okay – I know there are a number of you out there that are saying, "Whoa – if I wore a suit to my job interview at a construction company (heavy equipment company, trucking company, etc.) they would laugh me out of the building. That may be true, actually probably would be true. In those cases I would dress several levels above what you expect to see in the office. Blue jeans and t-shirts are the accepted office apparel? Then I would opt to wear a pair of clean and well-pressed khakis and a collared shirt. If business casual is the dress code (khakis and collared shirts), I suggest you wear a pair of slacks, a white or light blue shirt and a tie. Perhaps even a sports coat.

I once managed a training center, where my instructors taught classes to individuals who installed large telephone systems, computers, telephones, etc. The students were classic blue-collar workers, many of whom were pretty rough around the edges. Dress code for my instructors was business casual; most wore khakis, collared shirts and ties – their choice – but most didn't wear ties.

Occasionally I had to replace an instructor who had retired or moved on. The ideal candidate for the instructor position came from the ranks of our installers, because the technical ability and having "been there in the trenches" were critical to their knowledge, credibility and success. When I interviewed candidates, their dress ranged from dirty blue jeans to suits and ties. I have to admit, my impressions were formed quickly, notwithstanding I knew the ideal candidate's dress was less important than his technical skills and experience. If I recall correctly, through the years, I didn't hire any of the candidates who showed up in dirty blue jeans. I'd guess my hiring was pretty evenly divided between the candidates who wore suits and those who wore business casual clothing.

Having said that, may I share a story a friend shared with me? He was helping a Public Relations executive find work. The PR guy had several interviews with a dot. com-type software company for a six-figure position. Finally the call he was hoping for came: the CEO wanted to have lunch with him at an upscale restaurant. He was excited for the opportunity and knew he was on the threshold of ending his job search and going to work for a premier company.

Because he felt the work environment at the company was pretty casual, he had worn slacks, a sports coat and tie to both of his previous interviews. None of the managers with whom he interviewed wore ties – they were dressed in khakis and collared shirts. He had decided to dress like the company's managers for his meeting with the CEO – business casual. But he was uncertain enough about his decision that he called my friend to get his input. My friend strongly recommended the candidate wear his interview suit. They discussed and debated the issue at length, but the more my friend recommended a suit, the more firm the candidate became in his position of dressing more casually. He did agree to wear a tie, which he felt was a huge concession.

The day of the lunch interview finally came. The candidate got to the restaurant early and waited excitedly for the CEO to arrive. Imagine his shock – and discomfort – when the CEO walked through the restaurant doors wearing an expensive suit, gleaming white shirt and conservative red tie! When they shook hands, the candidate noticed expensive gold cuff links on the CEO's monogrammed shirt sleeves. They exchanged small talk on the way to their table. Once settled, the following conversation ensued:

> CEO: "I reviewed your resume and was very impressed with your education and experience. My managers spoke highly of your professionalism and capabilities. I know how PR executives are always concerned with appearances, so I wanted to show you how much I respected you as a candidate by wearing my best suit for our meeting today."

> The candidate knew he was toast. Thinking quickly, he said, "Well, thank you – you are most kind to say that. I know your company has a business casual dress code, so I dressed this way so I wouldn't make you feel uncomfortable. It seems we out-guessed one another!"

Nice try. The PR candidate didn't get the job, most likely because he made the wrong wardrobe decision.

Personally, I would prefer to risk being a little overdressed to being dressed too casually for an interview.

Questions

If you do nothing else I recommend in this chapter, pay particular attention to this next section and follow it to the letter. I will say that again, just to add emphasis:

If you do nothing else I recommend in this chapter, you should pay particular attention to this next section and follow it to the letter.

Before your interview, you should try to come up with as many questions as you think may be asked during the interview. Focus first on the job description and requirements you read in the job ad. How do you stack up against the requirements for the position? What questions might be asked of you as they relate to the position? If you were the hiring manager, what questions would you ask a candidate for this position?

Another source of questions is the Internet. Google things like: *Questions asked in HR interviews, Questions asked in sales interviews*, etc. You'll be surprised at the wealth of information available on the Internet on those topics. Some of the sites even provide recommended answers to the questions. You'll also get more information if you add the term *entry level* in your search string.

Once you have identified your list of questions, write them down. And then – and this is important – once you have written down the questions, **write down the answers**! This is the time to do that – when there is no pressure on you. Think each question through, think about the best answer possible, and write it down. Don't just *think* it out, but *write* it out. This gives you the opportunity to work out sentences and present your answer in the most powerful way possible.

Be honest in your answers. Also – look for ways you can answer the question that will make your hiring manager realize you would bring a lot of value to their company if they hire you.

The questions you write down and then answer should fall into two categories:

• Generic questions about your background and experience

• Questions specific to the job itself

Following are some of the generic questions I wrote down. I had a rather lengthy list of these questions (about 30) I reviewed before each job interview. Initially it took me quite a bit of time to come up with the answers, but since I wrote them down, they became a "study guide" for me before each interview. It was easy to run down the list of questions and refresh my memory.

Generic Questions

Question: Tell me about a time when you:

1. …had a difficult situation with a co-worker, fellow student or instructor.

Answer: "A few years ago we got a new director of legal recruiting at my firm. Andrea was a hard driving, get-it-done-at-any-cost leader. She was a tremendous recruiter, finding exceptional talent for our organization. However, sometimes, in her zeal to bring the best talent into the firm, she made offers that caused problems for the existing workforce (or more particularly, for management!). For example, at our firm, we awarded the title of Senior Associate to those attorneys who had at least five years legal experience, two of which had to be at our law firm.

To get top talent, Andrea would sometimes extend offers to experienced attorneys with the promise that they would come into the firm as a Senior Associate. Since these candidates didn't have two years' experience with our firm, bringing them in as Senior Associates was unfair to experienced attorneys already at our firm who were waiting to complete two years with the firm so they could become Senior Associates.

I spoke with Andrea and listened to her reasons for wanting and needing to bring these individuals in as Senior Associates, and she had some good reasons. I explained why it was posing problems for the firm – that existing employees were upset, that her offers violated firm policy, it created inequitable situations for existing employees, etc.

As we discussed possible solutions, it was apparent to me that our existing policy made it difficult for Andrea to attract top talent to the firm, and we prized top talent. I decided it was time we over-hauled our long-standing policy about requiring two years within our firm to be promoted to Senior Associate. I made a case to our Executive Committee, and the change was approved."

Debrief: Note that when I described the difficult situation. I didn't throw my co-worker under the bus – painting her as difficult to work with (which, by the way, she was!), but rather I presented her as someone passionate about her job and her drive to be successful (which, by the way, she was!). I let the hiring manager know I was flexible, open to discussion, willing to change for the right reasons. At the same time, I let the hiring manager know I felt rules and policies were important, but that the needs of the business came first, and I was willing to make changes if necessary.

2. …wrote a report that was well received.

Answer: "A couple years ago, at my recommendation, our firm competed to earn a spot in *Fortune's Top 100 Companies in America to Work For*. Part of the process was to have fifty percent of our randomly selected employees complete a fairly extensive survey.

We didn't win. But as part of our feedback, we were provided a synopsis of our employees' responses to the survey, categorized in about every imaginable way possible: by length of time with the firm, men / women, age, by specific minority, job family (attorney, secretary, paralegal, etc.), etc.

I wrote a multi-page report on the results of the survey. I highlighted areas the firm scored the highest, and what I thought we were doing that caused high ratings in each of those areas. I also identified the areas we were weakest, expressed my thoughts about why we were weak in those areas, and made proposals about how to strengthen those areas.

I presented the paper first to our Executive Committee and then to the firm in a Town Hall meeting. The Executive Committee expressed appreciation for the thorough presentation and boiling down the statistics into useable data. The Town Hall meeting generated tremendous discussion and great ideas on how to improve the firm."

Debrief: This answer allowed the hiring manager to see that I was proactive (I recommended that the firm participate in the contest) and had the ability to analyze and present data in a clear and concise manner.

Additional generic questions to prepare answers for might include:

Question: Tell me about a time when you:

3. …had to make a difficult decision with limited facts.
4. …when you set your sights too high (or too low!).
5. …had a new boss, co-worker, fellow student or professor whose trust you had to gain.
6. …had to deal with an angry customer.
7. …overcame a major obstacle.
8. …when you had competing priorities and not enough time to do them all. How did you solve the problem?
9. …had to resolve a conflict between two co-workers who reported to you.
10. …persuaded team members to do something your way.
11. …creatively solved a problem.
12. …anticipated potential problems and prepared for them.
13. …used good judgment to solve a major problem.

Since you're a recent college grad (or soon will be), you may encounter some of these questions:

• Why did you select (name of the university you attended)?
• What was your favorite course? Why?

• Did you have a favorite teacher? If so – what did s/he do that appealed to you?

• Why did you select _____ as a major?

• If we were to ask your professors to describe you, what three adjectives would they use?

• What extra-curricular activities did you participate in during your college career?

• Did you have an opportunity to demonstrate leadership in any situation during your college years?

• What do you want to be doing in five years?

And if you had an internship or two, here are a few questions you might anticipate:

• What was the most important lesson you learned as an intern?

• Who was the most influential mentor you had during your internship? Why – what made them effective?

• Tell us about the top two or three experiences you had as an intern.

• Was there anything you did as an intern that you were particularly proud of?

• Knowing what you know now, would you have done anything different as an intern? If so, what?

For a list of other behavior-based interview questions, just Google that phrase (behavior-based interview questions) and you'll get a number of questions to think about! And – Google the phrase entry-level interview questions, and you'll hit a veritable treasure trove (isn't the Internet great?!)

Job-Specific Questions

If you have any experience in the industry you're entering, you can expect job-related questions. The list of potential job-specific questions are endless, but here are a few types of questions that you might end up fielding, depending on the position for which you are interviewing and depending on any experience you may have.

Tell me about a time when you:

> 14. … took a sales area that had been under-producing and made it produce.
> 15. … solved a difficult personnel problem.
> 16. … had to discipline a problem employee.
> 17. …debugged a difficult software problem.
> 18. …managed a construction project.
> 19. …were responsible for project managing a multi-million dollar project.

And so forth. Note that "Tell me about a time when you…" and "Help me understand how you handled…" questions are pretty popular now. They allow the interviewer to discern if you have had experience in the areas that are specific to a particular job, and how you handled yourself in certain situations. Of course, if you have no prior job experience you will likely not be asked these kinds of questions.

You should also expect more philosophical-type questions:

> 20. If we hire you, what kind of employee will you be for us?
> 21. If I asked the people who worked with you what kind of employee you were, what would they say?
> 22. If you owned this company, what direction would you want the company to go in?

As important as some of these questions are, the very **most important questions** for you to focus on **are the questions you hope they won't ask** -- the ones you have the weakest answer for. *Hoping they won't ask those questions is not a good interview strategy!* Better to develop an answer you can live with, that will allay any (or most of the) concerns of the interviewer now, when you're not on the hot seat. While those questions are probably as numerous as there are candidates – we all seem to have at least one area of weakness – here are the types of questions you should be able to answer:

"You graduated last year and still haven't found a job. Why do you think that is?"

"You don't have nearly as much experience as some of the other candidates for this position. Why should we hire you?"

"Can you explain these gaps in your employment history?"

"Why did you leave this company after only a few months?"

These are the kinds of questions you need to be doubly prepared to answer in an interview. **Preparation up front is key to surviving this mine field**. Perhaps you have good answers to those questions; if that's the case, then you should work out your answers ahead of time. Perhaps your answers are less than satisfying to you; if that's the case, you need to massage them to make sure they will pass muster.

Don't lie. But how do you address the question: "Why did you leave this company after only a few months?" if the real answer is you got fired for poor performance?

Here are two possible answers to the above question:

I was fired for poor performance.

Or

It's very hard for me to talk about this. When I took the job shortly after I graduated, it appeared to be a great fit for my skills and background. But once I got into the job, I discovered that I was in way over my head – I really didn't have the knowledge and skills necessary to do the job. That became apparent very quickly. If the company would have had time to train me or work with me, I am sure I could have come up to speed. As it was, they needed someone to be able to hit the ground running. It was a mutual decision that I leave.

What questions do I hope they won't ask??

So – which answer would you prefer giving? I know which one I would prefer hearing as a hiring manager! Even though the second answer would give me a little concern, I am by nature a pretty fair-minded person, and can see how something like that could happen.

An important concept to keep in mind is that you must sell yourself! You are the product, and the hiring manager is the customer. Look for opportunities to answer questions in the most positive, advantageous-for-the-customer way possible.

I had a friend who had been unemployed for several years. On paper, he looked like a great candidate – he had a Bachelor's degree in electrical engineering and an MBA. He had a decade of experience in the field in which he was seeking employment. On paper, he was as good a candidate as you could hope for. He had many interviews, but was never the selected candidate.

One day after he learned he hadn't gotten yet another job, I proposed we do a mock interview. In preparation for the interview, I asked him to write down all the questions he could remember from his most recent interview as well as any others he could remember from previous interviews.

He came by my house with a fair number of questions. I told him to answer the questions as he did in the interviews, to the best of his recollection, and I started asking him the questions. The second question I asked him was:

"Have you ever used XYZ software?"

"No."

"That's it? You didn't say anything else?"

"No."

I thought I found a clue as to why he wasn't getting any of the jobs for which he'd interviewed, so I pursued that question a little further. I asked him if he was familiar with the XYZ software, and he said yes, of course, that it was one of the more common software packages in his line of work, but that he'd never used it before. I asked if there were similar software packages that did the same thing and if he had used them. He assured me that was the case – they were critical to the achievement of the work he did. So the better answer to the software question is:

> "No, I've not used XYZ software before, but I have used ABC and DEF software packages, which do the same thing. I am very adept at software, and there's no question in my mind that I could come up to speed on XYZ software very rapidly."

As we went through his list of questions, his responses to many of them were similar to the example I provided above. Yet, even the questions he answered positively were answered briefly and sparingly, with no effort to sell himself or his abilities.

Finally, one of my favorite questions to ask candidates is:

> • We have a number of excellent candidates for this position. Why should we hire you?

If you are asked this question, do not be humble. **Tell the hiring manager what you will do for them if they hire you**:

> "You should hire me because I am the best! You're looking for a new member of your robotics team. Having just graduated, I lack experience, but I also have the benefit of having recently taken four advanced robotics classes where I learned the most up-to-date, cutting-edge technology advances in robotics. I am sure I can use that knowledge, coupled with the experience of my team mates, to make some wicked advancements in your robotics program. I would love to put my knowledge to work in your organization, and I know you won't regret hiring me."

While writing one of my other jobs books, I interviewed a woman for an HR position. While she had the basic skills and qualifications we were seeking, she wasn't the most qualified candidate. When I asked her that question ("We have some strong candidates for this position -- why should we hire you?") she sat up tall, looked me in the eye and said:

> "*No one* will work as hard as I will work, and *no one* will be as passionate as I am about this job! I love this work and will give it my very best."

What's not to like about that answer?! By the way – I hired her…and she has been a tremendous employee!

My Least-Favorite Questions

There are two more questions that you will almost assuredly run into if you do much interviewing. They are questions I am not fond of, but they seem almost like a rite of passage for interviewers and candidates. Those questions are:

- Tell me about your strengths

- Tell me about your weaknesses

If I could ban two questions from the interview arena (aside from illegal ones), it would be these two. I think they show a lack of imagination and may indicate poor interviewing skills. Alas, I can almost guarantee you will run into one or the other, if not both of these questions. So it's best to be prepared for them.

The answer to the first question about your strengths should be evident: your strengths just happen to be exactly what the employer is looking for! You tailored your resume to the key elements of the job and that helped you get the interview. Carry that tailoring into the interview. You can't lie, of course, but you can accentuate the positive. Since we've spoken about robotics positions a bit, let's continue with that field.

"Well, Bob, I think one of the things that makes me stand out from other candidates – especially other recent grads – is how well I did in all my programming classes. I aced my Java, PLC/HMI, C, Basic C#, and C++ programming classes, and in fact I was asked to run several of the lab sessions for Java, since I understood it so well. I know from our discussions that those are critical skills for this position, and I am confident in my skills in those areas."

Now, to my least favorite of these two least favorites: "Tell me about your weaknesses." For years, common counsel was to make a weakness appear to be a strength that will appeal to the employer:

"Well, I guess I tend to work too many hours – sometimes I get so caught up in the job that I spend more time at work than I probably should."

Or

"I guess I am a perfectionist, and sometimes I am not as patient with others who aren't."

Most interviewers will see through answers like those as a make-your-weakness-appear-as-a-strength tactic. I would prefer to answer the weakness question with a weakness that has nothing to do with the job for which I am applying.

For example, my brother-in-law once asked me how to handle the weakness question if he were to run into it during an interview. He had a successful career with the Marines as a Public Relations officer, and was transitioning to private industry. Most of the jobs for which he was applying were state-side and had no need of dealing with foreign governments or non-English-speaking people. The weakness we decided he would share was:

"Well, I guess my greatest weakness is that I find it difficult to keep my train of thought and a good word flow when I am speaking through an interpreter."

So, while they may not be my favorite questions, expect to run into them during your interviews, and prepare accordingly.

The Unasked Questions

Regardless of the specific questions asked, whether they are generic or job-related – bear one thing in mind – all the questions are designed to answer the following questions:

- Will this person add value to my organization?

- Can this candidate solve this very important problem I have at this time in my organization?

- Can this fellow help me out?

- Will this candidate fit into our culture and the team with which he or she will be working?

More on Questions

There is another set of questions you should prepare: questions to ask your potential employer during the interview. Surely there are questions you will have about the job – think of around a half a dozen questions to ask your interviewer. Write them down and bring them with you to the interview. Some possible questions include:

- What do you expect the successful candidate to accomplish in their first six months on the job?

- What do you think are the key attributes of the candidate who will be most successful in this job?

- Why is this position vacant?

- When do you think you will be making a decision?

These questions should be written down on a padfolio or pad of paper that you will be taking to your interview. More on that in the next chapter.

Don't make this feel like an inquisition for the hiring manager. If the interview goes long, don't ask all your questions – ask the one or two that are uppermost on your mind. Don't extend the interview by a half hour asking your questions.

Note, by the way, that none of these questions has anything to do with benefits, vacation time, or salary. Your first interview is not the place to ask these questions. Asking those questions during the initial interview signals you are concerned about what's in it for you, not what you can do for their company.

If you will spend time doing and bearing in mind the things I have covered in this chapter, you will be prepared for your interview. That preparation will help you be confident as you arrive for your interview. And speaking of your interview, it's time to talk about interviews.

Before the Interview checklist

_____ Use my network to see if anyone in my network knows the person I will be interviewing with.

_____ Research the companies I will be interviewing with – learn about them.

_____ Dress for success – don't let a costume malfunction cost me a job!

_____ Before my interview, think of all the questions I might be asked. Write down the questions, then write down the answers. I can use this as a study guide for future interviews.

_____ What questions do I hope they won't ask? Prepare ahead of time for them

_____ If I am asked about my greatest weakness, share something that has nothing to do with the job I am seeking!

_____ Prepare a list of questions to ask the hiring manager at the end of my interview.

The Interview

You don't win the silver medal, you lose the gold medal.
– Nike commercial

Game time!

The time for practice and drills is over – you're stepping onto the gridiron, diamond, pitch, field, and mat. You've arrived – now it's time to shine.

First of all – congratulations for earning an interview. All your preparation has brought you to this point…now is not the time to choke.

When you are preparing for your interview, keep the **20-20-20 rule** in mind. In case you've never heard of the 20-20-20 rule, here it is broken down:

When you arrive for an interview, remember:

> • the first 20 feet,

> • the first 20 seconds,

> • the first 20 words.

This is where you will make your first impression – make the most of it.

Let's talk a little about each of those elements:

The first 20 feet. What happens during the first twenty feet? To begin with, you are establishing the first impression for all who meet you. Here are a few things I can think of:

- You're on time (or not).

- You smile pleasantly.

- You are wearing your interview suit, and look like a million bucks – you certainly look the part.

The first 20 seconds. How about:

- You greet the executive assistant or HR specialist professionally and politely.

- You sit like a professional (not sprawled on the couch, not reclining in a chair, etc.)

- You seem calm, cool and collected.

- You shake hands firmly.

- You make eye contact and smile at all those you meet.

The first twenty words.

- Your greeting is genuine and sincere.

- You remember – and use – people's names.

• You appear calm, your speech isn't overly informal, and you seem like a pleasant person.

So – pay attention to the first twenty feet, seconds and words.

Following are a few pointers gleaned through years of interviewing candidates for positions, from working with hiring managers and human resources departments.

Dress for Success!

In a previous chapter I provided my thoughts on how you should dress for your interview. Be sure and put on your interview duds – you'll feel like a winner as you walk out of your house, and the proper clothing will help you feel confident as you arrive for your interview.

Location

This may seem ridiculous to mention, but be sure you know where you are going for your interview. When I was in high school and college, when I asked a girl on a date, if I didn't know where she lived I always made a trial run before our date, making sure I could find her home, how long it took to get there, etc.

And you should do the same when you have gotten an interview. Make sure you have the address of the company. In addition to knowing what time to be there, know well where you are to be – what building, what floor, who to ask for, etc. The day or two before your interview, drive by the building.

When I interviewed with the law firm I worked at, their offices were located in downtown Denver, on the 41st floor. The day before the interview, I drove downtown in rush-hour traffic (since my interview was the next day at 8:30am), found where to park, and then walked into the building. I took the elevator to the 41st floor. I timed all this, and from leaving my driveway to arriving at the 41st floor, it took me 55 minutes – so basically an hour.

THE INTERVIEW

The next day, I left my house at 6:30am – two hours before my interview. Since traffic wasn't quite as busy as the day before (since I left an hour earlier!), I got there in plenty of time – I had about an hour and fifteen minutes to burn before the interview.

Fortunately, I had brought my behavior-based questions with me, so I used the time to bone up on my answers and to practice them. I also had the job description, so I could refresh my memory about all the elements of my specialty they were looking for.

As the time for my interview approached, I left my car and walked to the building. I waited in the lobby the last ten minutes or so, then at about five minutes before my interview, I stepped on the elevator. I arrived at the reception desk about three minutes before my interview, and informed the receptionist I was there, and who I was to interview with.

Timing

Now, as you read that last few paragraphs, you might be thinking, "Dan's OCD is showing again!" And yes, you would be correct. But beyond that, **I cannot stress enough the importance of being on time to your interview**! Notice I said, "On time," not "Arrive early." I have to be honest, it annoys me to no end to have a candidate show up twenty or thirty minutes before the time for their interview. Often, I schedule interviews back to back. That means if you arrive twenty minutes early and my secretary calls me, you are interrupting someone else's interview. Also, even if I am not in an interview, believe me, I have plenty to do. I will not appreciate that you have arrived early. It does not signal to me your eagerness about the job – it mostly just annoys me. And it is never good to annoy the hiring manager.

As bad as arriving early, arriving late is worse. Through the years, I have had far too many candidates arrive late. Sometimes they call ahead to tell me they are stuck in traffic, or have gotten lost, or whatever. That softens the blow a bit, but it is not impressive. You see above how fixated I am about time. The fact that you are late may throw other interviews off. Or – I may interview you for half an hour instead of 45 minutes or an hour – I will short you, not the candidate after you.

If you are late for an interview, you have one strike against you before you even meet the hiring manager. If you arrive really early (ten to thirty minutes) you have about three quarters of a strike against you before you begin.

For those times when you are unavoidably late, it is good to have the company's main number as well as the number for the hiring manager with you the day of the interview. If you are running late, by all means call the hiring manager. But he or she may not be in their office – they may have other meetings, be interviewing other candidates, etc. If no one answers his or her phone, try hitting 0 and # during their voice mail message -- that will often transfer you to the hiring manager's secretary, who can get a message to the manager. If 0 # doesn't work, having the main number of the company allows you to reach the receptionist, who can then get you to the manager's secretary.

But bottom line is – don't be late. You've heard the axiom *Better late than never?* Well, when it comes to interviewing, I would say: *Better never late.*

Better never late!

Resume

When you arrive for your interview, you should have brought three to five copies of your resume with you. Carry them in a padfolio or along with a pad of paper so they don't get smudged or wrinkled. The padfolio / pad of paper also has the benefit of being something you can take notes on during your interview. This isn't a must, but I always like to interview candidates who take notes during interviews. We all like to think what we are saying is important or of interest to others.

You should bring multiple copies of your resume for a number of reasons:

1. Bring numerous copies since there may be more than one interviewer – team interviews are very popular these days.

2. The hiring manager may have forgotten to bring your resume to the interview.

3. Often, resumes that get cut and pasted into applications software are in plain text – no formatting, functional spacing between paragraphs, etc. The resume you have labored over (see the earlier chapter on resumes) to present just the right image is wasted!

4. It shows you are prepared and are courteous – that you think of others.

Whether you need them or not, I think it is a good sign of your preparation and professionalism if you arrive with resumes ready for your interviewers.

Business cards

When you meet your interviewers, ask each of them for a business card. When they are handed to you – look at them. This will give you a moment to see the name of each interviewer (did she say Aubrey or Audrey? Kathy or Cassie?).

People's names are important to them – use them in your interview. When Kathy asks you a question, respond with, "Thanks, Kathy, that's an intriguing question…" and then answer the question.

It's About the Company

This is something good for you to remember as you head into your interview – everything in the interview is about the company. That may seem odd – you may have been thinking it's all about you. That makes sense – they have called you, asked to interview with you, they have your resume and application. But believe me, it is all about the company, not all about you. **Your interviewers will be evaluating your answers against their checklist of needs**. If your answers don't show them how you will help them solve their problems, boost their sales, increase their customer service, protect the company, etc., you will not be hired.

They will most likely *not* ask you those specific questions. But they will be listening carefully to what you say and trying to determine if you are the answer to their problems. So remember that.

Let me give you an example. Here's a pretty innocent question:

- Tell me why you would like to work for our company.

If you answer something like, "I'd love to work for your company because having a job here would cut my commute in half. That's more time for me to spend with my family."

Now, there's nothing wrong with spending time with your family, but with an answer like that you missed a golden opportunity to establish yourself as the best candidate for this company. Compare that answer to this one:

"I have always admired your company, and when I read the job description, I realized I have skills and abilities that will help you meet your strategic goals this year."

Or this answer:

"Well, I read in the newspaper that you were expecting to bid on some new government contracts over the next few months. I have great strengths in that area, and thought my experience in that area would be able to help you immediately."

With the first answer, you may be on your way out the door (whether you know it or not), but using the second or third answers keeps you in the game, and the interviewers will be interested in learning just how you intend to help them meet their strategic goals or how your expertise in government bidding might help them.

The Interview

Now you're down to brass tacks. You've done all the preparation you can, from learning about the company, rehearsing answers to potential questions, dressing appropriately, arriving on time, etc. The spotlight's on, and you are on stage. Time to shine!

Often, as a warm-up question, interviewers will ask the vanilla question, "Can you tell us a little about yourself?" I think this is sort of an ice breaker, an opportunity to put you at ease. It is important to note that in response to this inquiry, most interviewers don't want to hear about your spouse, children, sports activities, hobbies, etc. They are really looking for how you can help them. Remember that – no matter how nice they are (and they may be exceptionally nice people!), what they are really looking for is whether or not you can add value to the organization, solve a problem for them or help them out in some way. All your answers should be given with those things in mind.

You can use this question to answer those unasked questions, and to set the tone for the rest of your interview. Here's an answer you might provide if you were a recent graduate seeking a position in robotics:

> "First of all – thank you for your time today. I know you are all very busy. In answer to your question: In May I graduated from the University of Southern California with a Bachelor's of Science degree in Electrical Engineering with specialization in robotics. I am looking for an opportunity to use my knowledge and the experience I gained through my studies in robotics and during an internship in robotics at SCL Enterprises. While I liked and did well in all my programming classes, Java and PLC/HMI were two of my favorites, and they've helped me become passionate about robotics. I am excited to enter the industry and use my learning and experience with a top-notch company. And that's me in a nutshell."

Look at what you just told the interviewer about yourself in about thirty seconds:

- You recently graduated from USC;

- You have an Electrical Engineering degree with specialization in robotics;

- You had an internship with SCL Enterprises

- You liked and did well in all your programming classes;

- Your favorite programming classes were Java and PLC/HMI;

- You're passionate about robotics.

And – did your response answer any of the following un-asked questions:

- Will this person add value to my organization?

- Can this candidate solve this very important problem I have at this time in my organization?

- Can this fellow help me out?

- Will this candidate fit into our culture and the team with which he or she will be working?

I think your answer addressed each of those questions in one way or another.

Listen. As you are asked questions, be sure and *listen to the entire question.* Don't be in such a hurry to answer that you cut the questioner off. I had an experience with a candidate like that – she just wouldn't let me finish a question before she jumped in with her answer. It was rather vexing for me. I am sure she was anxious to please and show that she really knew what she was talking about. But mostly it was off-putting.

If you don't understand a question – don't guess. Ask for clarification – there is no problem with that. Simply say, "I'm sorry, but I don't understand exactly what you are asking. Would you mind repeating the question?" Most interviewers will reword the question in a manner that will make it more understandable.

Don't be a Story teller! Now I will give you some advice I need to remind myself about often during interviews. **Get to the point when you answer questions**. I have a really bad habit of telling people the history of time when they ask me what time it is, and I frequently don't get around to ever telling them the time. If you find your answers wandering around, and it's taking you a long time to get to the point of the answer, economize and get to the answer. Better yet, if you know this is a practice of yours, studiously try to get to the point quickly. Watch your interviewers – if they are getting fidgety, or cut you off mid-answer, recalculate your answer strategy. Not to do so may mean your interview will not end well for you. Save the stories and charismatic answers for when you have the job.

Save the story telling the bedtime!

Dangerous Questions

There are questions you must watch out for, questions that may pose problems for you. No, they aren't necessarily the questions that highlight your areas of weakness – we talked in an earlier chapter about how to prepare for and answer those questions. The questions I am speaking about are those that may inadvertently show things you don't want hiring managers to see. Questions like:

> • "Tell us about a time you didn't get along with a co-worker."

When answering this question, don't throw your co-worker under the bus. If you do, it may signal to the hiring manager that you are difficult to work with, or not a team player. Focus on the positive things you did to get through the situation without damaging the relationship – we discussed that in the previous chapter. If the situation that comes to mind is really a negative one that puts you in a bad light no matter how you portray it, then select another situation where you and a co-worker didn't get along. If you have worked long enough, you probably have any number of examples from which you can draw, and of course, if you have prepared for this question, you'll have just the right answer to that question.

• "Tell us why you left your previous employment."

When answering this question, this is not the time to share what an idiot or jerk your former boss was, or the poor benefits package the company offered, even if those things are true. In a recent interview, a member of the interview team I was part of asked this question, and we were stunned to hear the candidate go on and on about the terrible, illegal things her boss was doing. If that wasn't enough, she went into great detail about a disciplinary meeting she was called into and the reasons she was being disciplined. Turns out, she didn't care for the way her supervisor handled the disciplinary meeting.

Next candidate please!

• "Tell us what you would do during the first six months you are here."

This is a great opportunity to share how hard you'll work, how committed to learning the organization you are, etc. It is not a time to point out the errors you think they have as an organization (even if they have expressed concern about the way they do some things). I interviewed a fellow once who basically trashed our company's compensation policy and told me how he would "clean things up" if he was to come to our company. I did not hire him.

Your End-of-Interview Questions

At the end of the interview, hiring managers will often ask if you have any questions. Now is the time to ask the questions you have already written down (in your padfolio or on a pad of paper) and brought with you to the meeting.

There are several reasons to write your questions down. First, during the stress or adrenaline rush of the interview, you may forget what those excellent questions were that you prepared before the interview. Second, I am generally a little put off by candidates who say, "No, I can't think of any questions for you." Really? You're not the least bit curious about this or that aspect of the job?

Often, during the course of the interview, many – or even all – your well-planned questions will be answered. That's okay; but if you have written down your questions, you can scan the questions on your pad of paper (letting the hiring manager know you really did put some thought into this interview) and say something like, "Well, I had a whole list of questions to ask you, but throughout our interview, you have answered all of them." However – you'll almost always have one question:

- "What are the next steps?"

This gives you the opportunity to find out where the company is in their hiring process, and when you might expect to hear back from them. Perhaps you are the first interview, or the last. Regardless, you should be able to learn when they will get back with you – whether for good or ill. It also provides you the opportunity to contact them if you do not hear back from them within a reasonable timeframe. Through the years, several candidates have tried a "trial close" on me. By that, I mean they asked me something like: "Can you tell me how I stack up against your other candidates?" or "After what you've seen today during our interview, do you feel I am your top candidate?" While as a former salesman, I appreciate this, as a hiring manager I am not a big fan of it. It puts me on the spot, and I don't care for that. Having said that, I know a number of individuals whom I respect greatly, who use this tactic and have had good results with it through the years. It's just not for me.

After the Interview
Congratulations – you survived! You can breathe a sigh of relief, and now the waiting begins.

When you get home, one of the first things you should do is sit down and write a **Thank-You note** to all those with whom you interviewed. (That's another reason to get business cards during the interview.) Some experts say this is another time for you to make your case as the best candidate. However, I think it should be just what the two words on the front of the card say: Thank You. Your message should be short and to the point, something along the lines of:

Dear Mr. Johnson,

Just a quick note to thank you for your time today. I know you are busy, and I appreciated the time you spent with me to help me learn more about Acme Engineering.

Thank you so much for your time and consideration. If I can answer any further questions for you, please don't hesitate to contact me.

Best Regards,

Daniel Quillen

This should be written on a professional-looking **Thank-you card**. And remember what your mother always said – "Use your best penmanship."

When I have mentioned this tactic to people with whom I am counseling about job hunting, invariably some ask, "Won't an e-mail be easier and just as effective?"

The answer is yes and no. Yes, it's easier; no, it's not just as effective. Anyone can take twenty seconds and fire off an e-mail, but a handwritten thank-you note separates you from the crowd. I'd guess about 30% of the candidates I have interviewed through the years have sent an e-mail thank you, but only 1% or 2% have sent a handwritten note. It's impressive to me. Will it make the difference? Not if you don't have the skills and qualifications required for the job. But if it's close between you and someone else, who knows? I don't think it hurts.

You might also contact those whose names you have provided as references, and let them know they may be contacted. Tell them about the job for which you have interviewed, and if you want them to accentuate anything about them as a candidate, ask them to mention that if they are so inclined.

Follow-Up

If you don't hear something right away, when is it too soon to follow up? Part of that depends on what the next steps were going to be for the hiring manager. If s/he told you that you were one of the first to be interviewed and it would take a couple weeks to get through the rest of the candidates, don't be calling a week after your interview looking for an update.

If, however, the hiring manager told you that you were one of the last interviews, and they should make a decision by the end of the week, then I think you can call on Tuesday of the following week if you haven't heard anything. Tuesday isn't pushy – calling the Friday the hiring manager said they would make the decision seems pushy to me. When you call on Tuesday, your message should be something like:

> Hello, Mr. Johnson, Dan Quillen here. I remember you mentioned you were hoping to make your decision on the HR Director position by last Friday, so I thought I would follow up to see if you have any further questions for me. Also, I just wanted to let you know I am still very interested in the position.

I can tell you from personal hiring experience that I am often unable to make a hiring decision in the timeframes I initially shared with candidates. Work gets busy, a candidate cancels and has to reschedule, and any number of other reasons.

But here's something to remember – just because getting hired by that company is at the top of your importance list, chances are pretty good that it gets easily supplanted in the hiring manager's business life – filling the position is the smoke on the horizon, and while that's important, the fire at his feet is going to take precedence every time.

Having said that, I think it's fine to check in occasionally until you're told someone else has the job (or until you get the job), but be careful – persistence is good – it shows you are interested in the job. However, there is a fine line between persistence and stalking.

Don't be a stalker!

If the manager seems evasive or quits returning your calls, assume the worst and move on. You might be pleasantly surprised, and s/he may call later than you expect to offer the job, or call you in for another interview, but don't make a nuisance of yourself. If the call comes and – sad day – you are not the chosen candidate, be professional in your response. Don't subject the caller to a litany of questions about why you weren't chosen. It is okay to express disappointment, but be completely professional. More than once I have hired someone who didn't work out, and I went to Candidate #2. Also – more than once I hired someone who didn't work out, but I didn't call Candidate #2 because they were a complete jerk when I initially called with the bad information. I've even had Candidate #2 hang up on me when I told them they were not chosen for the job! Poor form at best.

Telephone Interviews

May I say a word or two about phone interviews? In today's fast-paced business world, many first interviews are conducted by telephone. Earlier in this book, I cited the fact that I had 31 interviews while looking for a job. Actually, I had far more than that, but I only counted one interview per company. Of those 31 interviews, over half (16) were telephone interviews (one was an interview over Skype). Sometimes it was because of distance – the recruiter or HR professional with whom I was interviewing lived in a distant city. Other times, it was a preliminary or screening interview, even though the company was located in the same city as me.

Be sure and treat every interview with the importance it deserves – don't do any less preparation, don't be any less professional.

The Interview checklist

_____ I will pretend the hiring manager is as obsessive about time as Mr. Quillen is, and I will be on time for my interview – not twenty minutes early, not one minute late, but on time!

_____ I will be sure and dress appropriately for my job interview.

_____ Remember – the interview is not about me – it is about the company, and they will be looking to see if I will solve any problems for them, fit on their team, etc.

_____ Request business cards from all the interviewers.

_____ Remember my interviewers' names, and use them during the interview.

_____ Don't be a storyteller!

_____ Send a Thank You note after my interview – and just say, "Thank You!" (No further attempts to sell myself.)

_____ Be patient – don't follow up too soon.

_____ Don't be a stalker!

_____ Telephone interviews are real interviews!

Gatekeepers

Always be nice to secretaries. They are the real gatekeepers in the world.
– Anthony J. D'Angelo

During your job search, I can guarantee you will encounter **gatekeepers** – those that will do their best to keep you away from your intended target – the hiring manager -- and your ultimate target – a new job. In this chapter we'll discuss several of them, and how to overcome their best efforts to screen you out.

Applications Software

During your job search, you'll almost assuredly run into **applications software**. These sophisticated tools of Human Resource departments provide the first hoop for you to jump through in your quest to become an employee of many companies. Refusing to do so, or trying to game the system, will result in no interview and no job, regardless of how qualified you are.

Since you are just graduating, this may be a new experience for you. But it is one you'll likely not be able to avoid. During my recent job search, I submitted my application for 130 jobs. Of those jobs, approximately 115 of them funneled all applicants through applications software.

And what does this applications software do? At its basic level, it provides screening assistance for busy HR departments and hiring managers: it screens in some applicants, and screens out others. Let me provide several examples:

GATEKEEPERS

Let's say a company has advertised a job with the following minimum requirements:

> Must have a Bachelor's degree, Master's degree preferred. Must have PHR, SPHR and / or CEBS certification. Successful applicants will have a minimum of two years of experience in this field. Must have complete fluency in Spanish, including reading, writing and speaking.

The company's applications software will be programmed to ask a series of job-relevant questions. Samples of possible questions include:

1. How many years' experience do you have in XYZ field?
a. 0 to 1
b. 2 to 3
c. 4 to 5
d. more than 5

2. Do you have a Bachelor's degree?
a. Yes
b. No

3. Do you have a Master's degree?
a. Yes
b. No

4. This position requires fluency in Spanish. At what level are you fluent?
a. Reading, writing and speaking.
b. Reading only.
c. Speaking only.
d. Writing only.

5. Do you have current PHR, SPHR or CEBS certification?
a. Yes
b. No

All rather benign questions, wouldn't you agree? But an HR department or hiring manager can instruct the applications software to screen out those applicants whose answers indicate they don't meet the minimum requirements of the job. Your application may go no further than this faceless, nameless – and very effective – gatekeeper.

More sophisticated applications software also scan an applicant's resume for skills and experiences that are important to the hiring manager and required for the job. Like the example above, it can review your software in microseconds and accept – or reject -- your resume based on whether it finds certain key words and phrases. You could be the most qualified candidate for the position, but if your resume doesn't possess the correct words and phrases, it will be rejected, and your resume will never even make it to the hiring manager for her or his review. That's why in the Resumes chapter, I stressed using the company's words from the job description in your resume.

Don't believe me? Let me give you a very concrete example that happened to me.

Early in my job hunt, I found myself up late one night / early one morning. I was searching for work when I ran across a position that looked interesting, and began tailoring my resume. I printed off the job description, circled the critical elements, and then began tailoring away. While I had experience in most of the areas the job required, there were a few areas of experience I was short on. I decided to submit anyway. After readying my resume, I went to the applications software and uploaded my resume. **It was 2:46am** by the time I finally hit Submit.

Immediately I received an e-mail from the company, acknowledging my submission. Here is the e-mail (I added the **bolding**, and redacted the company's name):

****

From: _____ Company donotreply@trm.brassring.com
To: wdanielquillen@gmail.com
Date: **Mon, Jul 18, 2011 at 2:46 AM**
Subject: Your candidate reference number - _____ Company.

GATEKEEPERS

Thank you, W Quillen, for expressing interest in _____.

We have successfully received your submission to the following position(s): Training and Development Coordinator 18730BR

Your background, skills and experience will be reviewed against the position you have selected. Your resume will also remain on file for your use when exploring future _____ career opportunities.

As a world leader in defense electronics, _____ Company is committed to providing challenging and rewarding opportunities. Please continue to investigate other positions with _____ and submit your resume to those that are of interest.

Sincerely,

_____ Talent Acquisition Team

****

Ten minutes later, at 2:56am, I received the following e-mail:

****

From: AutomationManager@brassring.com Enterprise@trm.brassring.com
To: wdanielquillen@gmail.com
Date: **Mon, Jul 18, 2011 at 2:56 AM**
Subject: Regarding Your _____ Job Submission

Dear W,

Thank you for submitting your resume for the position of Training and Development Coordinator, Req ID 18730BR.

Your background and qualifications have been given careful review with respect to this position. Although you were not selected for this position, we appreciate your desire to expand your career. Please check your Job Submission status to get the most updated status of other _____ opportunities to which you have applied.

Please continue to investigate other job postings with _____ and apply to any that are commensurate with your background and experience.

Again, thank you for your interest in _____.

Sincerely,

_____ Talent Acquisition Team

****

Note the statement in the second paragraph:

> **Your background and qualifications have been given careful review with respect to this position**. Although you were not selected for this position, we appreciate your desire to expand your career.

Forgive my skepticism, but I seriously doubt there was a recruiter / member of the HR team sitting at their desk at 2:46am on July 18, 2011, just waiting for resumes to pop into their e-mail inbox so they could *carefully* review them. (It is true that many members of HR departments are over-worked, but I suspect that's not what was happening here.) The "careful review" of my background and qualifications was in all likelihood performed by applications software – in this case Brass Ring, one of the leading application software systems in the industry.

But don't dismay. If you follow the suggestions I have made throughout this book, it will increase your chances of getting past this initial gatekeeper.

Another important thing to keep in mind is this: follow the instructions. Just like the need to be obedient in elementary school:

- raise your hand before you speak;
- walk, don't run;
- no cutting in line;
- put your name on your paper;
- etc.

You must follow the instructions presented to you in the applications software. Several critical instructions I have seen include:

1. Complete and thorough responses to the following questions are necessary in order to be considered for this vacancy and move to the next step in the recruitment process.

2. Please provide a detailed description of your job responsibilities for each position. Do not type, "See Resume."

In various forms, I ran across item Number 1 above in numerous applications frontends during my job search, the last of which was with the entity at which I was hired – the City of Aurora, Colorado. It is a standard instruction we put at the beginning of most applications. After reviewing hundreds of applications for the City, it is amazing to me how many candidates ignore that instruction, and it almost always seems to mean they ignore Number 2 above also. And I'll tell you how the screeners in my department handle those applications: they reject them with the notation: "Did not follow application instructions."

Okay, so you're a maverick and like to blaze your own trail. I get that. I understand that. But don't do it during the application process.

Human Resources Departments

HR departments also serve as gatekeepers through whom you (or your resume) must pass to get to the hiring managers. In many companies, HR organizations screen resumes for hiring managers, handing off to them the top three to six resumes that come in. Each department does it a little differently – some do it manually, some use applications software to do the first screen, then they do the next level of screening.

Fill out all applications completely!

At this stage of the process, think of HR departments as human application software: they screen resumes, searching for those that meet the minimum requirements of the position – education, experience, certifications, etc., often culling the stack of resumes first using those criteria. Once they have a more manageable pile of resumes to review, then they review looking for specific experience, accomplishments – things that say, "This candidate is Top Notch," etc.

Executive Assistants

Executive assistants can provide a formidable hurdle to get around as you try to gain access to the hiring manager. They are good at protecting their manager from intrusions throughout the day, and in many cases, s/he will lump you into the **Intrusions** category.

Executive assistants come into play, of course, only if you have gotten to the hiring manager level of the hiring process. This can happen any of several ways:

> • you are aware of who the hiring manager is through your network of friends and professional colleagues;

> • you have found the hiring manager's name by calling the company, checking out their website, or even from the job ad itself;

> • the hiring manager has posted a position on Facebook, Twitter, LinkedIn, etc.

> • You have interviewed with, or been contacted by the hiring manager for the position in question;

> • any creative way you can find him / her.

Regardless of how you are in possession of the hiring manager's name, the executive assistant stands ready to stymie your efforts to get through to your potential manager. And they are often very good at what they do.

And, before I give you the tip that will help you get past this Gatekeeper, let me tell you that executive assistants are far more powerful and influential than many people realize. Often, hiring managers will ask their executive assistant what they think about a candidate. If you have been short with him or her, rude, frustrated, etc., you can bet she'll share that insight – *and it will be listened to*. First of all, I understand you should be polite and professional to everyone you meet. But it is imperative that you are on your very best behavior (as my mother would say) in all your dealings with the hiring manager's executive assistant.

Recently, we were interviewing candidates for positions at my office. We interviewed a number of candidates, and invited four back for a second interview. All these candidates were strong, but there were two that were exceptionally strong, and we were frankly having a difficult time deciding between the two.

That is, until we spoke with our receptionist. She shared with us that one of those two candidates had been pretty nasty with her when she arrived for the interview. That made our decision easy – we hired the other top candidate.

Back to the executive secretary Gatekeeper…

That isn't to say you shouldn't try to get around their gatekeeping efforts. Here is the key: while most executive assistants work hard, they often work 8:00am to 5:00pm, while their managers may be working 7:30am to 6:00pm or later. So here's the hint – call before formal business hours or call after the workday has ended. Call during the lunch hour. While the executive assistant may be off during those times, the hiring manager often is not. If you try at 7:30am and the executive assistant answers, then try after hours – 5:30pm, for example.

Gatekeepers checklist

_____ There will be a number of gatekeepers who will try to thwart my quest for employment.

_____ Follow the rules when submitting through applications software – not to do so could cost me a shot at the job.

_____ Secretaries can be formidable, but I must be polite and professional with them – always!

_____ To get around a particularly effective executive secretary, call before or after normal work hours, or during lunch.

Are You Too Young for this Job?

Age is an issue of mind over matter. If you don't mind, it doesn't matter.
— Mark Twain

In a word, no: you are *not* too young for the job you're applying for!

However, you may be facing age discrimination because of your youth. Remember in the early chapter on Millennials where I listed some of the unflattering stereotypes that are sometimes applied to those of your generation? Even though you don't like and frequently reject labels, the fact is that some hiring managers may hold some of those preconceived notions about younger workers. As a refresher, here are those unflattering stereotypes of Millennials:

- Narcissistic
- Lazy
- Painfully / brutally honest
- Ladened with trophies, often undeserved (participation trophies)
- Can't take constructive criticism
- You want it all now — VP, corner office, etc.

So — let's concoct a few things you can say at the end of an interview that address some of those unflattering stereotypes that the hiring manager may have of you / Millennials. As you near the end of your interview and the hiring manager asks if you have any questions, you can say something like:

"Well, yes, I do have a few things I'd like to add. I am going to guess that I am much younger than some of the other applicants for this position. And perhaps I have less experience than some of those candidates. But let me tell you a little about myself that may not have come through in our interview:

Even though I have just graduated from college, I understand I have a lot to learn. While my head is full of theory and hypotheticals, I understand the real world is sometimes a bit different than the academic environment. I am looking forward to learning how I can contribute in the real world, while being open to those who can teach me the differences between the real world and academia."

(That addresses any concerns they may have that you're going to come in as a prima donna with all your college learning. And – you're not going to be offered a vice presidency after you've been at the company for six months!)

"My parents taught me I had to work for what I earn – no one is going to hand me something on a silver platter. I have to work hard, produce top-quality outputs and do it with a smile on my face. And since I don't have as much experience as my co-workers will have, I am going to have to work twice as hard."

(So much for coming across as lazy and that you expect to get a trophy for merely showing up!)

"I've learned through the years that you catch more flies with honey than with vinegar. I know some of my peers can be pretty honest in their criticisms, but I also know that people deserve a break."

(So much for being brutally honest, to the point of being unkind.)

"I want to learn, and I hope that my co-workers and bosses will be willing to help me understand when I need to change, perform better, or just simply need to do things differently. I welcome feedback and want it so I can be a better contributor to my team and the company."

(This addresses the fear that you cannot take constructive criticism.)

You may not use all of those thoughts, but you should be prepared to share those you think may be necessary to counter some of the negative stereotypes that are out there. And remember – you can also accentuate the positive:

- Confident
- Creative
- Connected
- Technologically savvy
- Interested in meaningful work (work that provides more than just a paycheck)
- Open to Change

"I am really excited about the possibilities this position offers. I know that as I work with my team, we'll be able to help each other's creative juices begin flowing. I'd love to apply my knowledge of the latest software to some of the problems you mentioned your team is wrestling with – I think we can do some great things."

And finally, remember the woman I hired, even though she didn't have as much experience as some of the other candidates we interviewed? Here's what she said:

"No one will work as hard as I will work, and *no one* will be as passionate as I am about this job! I love this work and will give it my very best."

Don't be afraid to counter negative stereotypes or sell my strengths!

A number of years ago, one of my sons was interested in working for a TV studio. He had only recently graduated from high school, had one semester of college, and had a real interest in making the technology portion of theater and television his career. He had worked on the sound and lighting crews for plays for several years in high school – it was his passion. While he had no paid positions in the field, he did have a lot of voluntary experience and he listed his (extensive) volunteer experience on his otherwise rather skimpy (lacking experience) resume. It was enough to tip the decision in his favor, and he secured the job and was finally able to get paid for working in a field he was passionate about. Following is his resume from that time period.

W. Michael Quillen
Address, e-mail and phone numbers

Summary

BA candidate with nearly four years of experience in creating sound design and operating sound, lighting boards and shop time. Worked with equipment such as Machie, ETS Express, Shure, Audio-Technica, and others. Also has knowledge about and experience with different soundboards and systems. Over 800 hours of shop time recorded over 3 years. Theater experience includes performing in outstanding plays such as *Chess, Into the Woods, Secret Garden* and *Evita*, and Stage Manager for *Little Shop of Horrors*.

Student intern for four months working in Lucent Technologies' business television studio. Performed a variety of roles in that position, including cameraman, sound and light board designer and operator.

Skills include leadership, precision, professionalism, and the flexibility to adapt to difficult situations. Proficient in MS Word and experienced in Excel. Fluent in Czech and Slovak.

1. Experience in Sound and Light

Show	Position	Location
Grease	Designed and Operated Board	Eaglecrest HS
Chess	Designed	Eaglecrest HS
Anything Goes	Assisted in Operating Board	Eaglecrest HS

Count Dracula	Assisted in Design	Eaglecrest HS
Evita	Co-Designer	Eaglecrest HS
Into the Woods	Designed	Eaglecrest HS
Peter Pan	Designed and Operated Board	Eaglecrest HS
Prelude to a Kiss	Assisted in Design	Eaglecrest HS
Secret Garden	Assisted in Design	Eaglecrest HS
Steel Magnolias	Designed and Operated Board	Eaglecrest HS
The Mystery of Edwin Drood	Designed and Operated Board	Eaglecrest HS
The Wayside Motor Inn	Designed and Operated Board	Eaglecrest HS
Working	Assisted in Design	Eaglecrest HS
Lost In Yonkers	Assisted in Light Design	Eaglecrest HS
Rumors	Operated Board	So. Utah University
Business Television Studio	Sound and Light Board Intern	Lucent Technologies

Awards and Honors

Outstanding Theater Student award for 1997-1998

Outstanding Theatre Student for junior class (1996-1997)

The Michael Landon Award (All-around outstanding Performing Arts Student)

Outstanding Choir Student for senior class (1997-1998)

Worked on a Foreign Exchange program with French Theatre Company (1998)

Highest Thespian Points in Cherry Creek School District (1996-1997)

One of three students selected to participate in interviewing candidates for new teacher positions at Eaglecrest HS

Voluntary representative for the Church of Jesus Christ of Latter-day Saints in the Czech Republic and Slovakia

As you can see, this young man (my son) didn't have a lot of experience in a paying job in the field he was seeking, but he showed all the volunteer work he had done during his high school years and one semester of college. He was competing against a number of other youth applying for the same job, but his passion and interest shone through and he got the job. I know you're curious what he ended up doing with all that sound experience…he is now a litigation attorney in Washington state!

Are You Too Young for this Job? checklist

_____ I may run into age discrimination. I can proactively battle that by providing examples of my work ethic, skills, etc.

_____ Accentuate the positive – my energy, passion and desire to work in this field; let them shine through!

_____ Include any experience I have that is relevant to the job for which I am applying – even volunteer work.

Temp Agencies – Yes or No?

If you're not willing to work hard, let someone else do it. I'd rather be with someone who does a horrible job, but gives 110% than with someone who does a good job and gives 60%. – Will Smith

I am often asked whether job seekers should look into / use temporary agencies. That's an easier question asked than answered, but I will try.

I have two arguments **against** agencies (but be sure and read further to see why I *like* them!). The first is that if you do find a temporary job, you will not be able to spend forty hours each week looking for other full-time work. The second is that if you go from temporary job to temporary job, it may dilute your resume. When I have considered candidates that had a history of temporary or contract jobs, I didn't count that time as equal to work with the same employer in a full-time employee capacity. That's particularly true with job seekers with lots of experience; but for recent college grads, that's not such a big issue.

I have found that sometimes people will register with a couple of agencies, and then sit back and wait for them to do the work of finding a job for them. That's bad – you can use them as a tool in your job search, but they should not be the only tool you are using in your job hunt.

Those concerns notwithstanding, I also have to say I think temporary agencies are often overlooked by job hunters, and they are a viable way to:

1. Bring a few bucks in while you seek full-time employment,
2. Get your foot in the door of a company.
3. Keep your skills honed for that perfect job.

Let me discuss each of those items:

Bring a few bucks in the door. Depending on how sound you are financially as you prepare to leave school, you may truly need to take anything that will help bring a few dollars in the door. If you are like many graduating college students, you are stretched pretty thin financially. Having the funds coming in from a temporary job may make all the difference.

Generally speaking, you won't make nearly as much working for a temp agency as you would if you were working at the company as a full-time employee – the company has to pay your salary, as well as extra to add to the bottom line for the temp agency.

Get your foot in the door. As an employer, I like using temporary agencies to hire talent. It allows me a "test drive" of an employee before determining if they have the skills, work ethic and attitude I want and expect of my employees. Through the years, we have had many temporary employees come through the door who we eventually hired as a full-time employee. Conversely, there were also a few times where we thought, "Good heavens – I am so glad we didn't hire her!"

Keep your skills honed. Face it, the longer you are away from school / an internship, the more likely it is that your skills will begin to suffer. And whether that is the case or not, from the perspective of employers, they will be concerned that a long time out of school or off the job may impact the contribution you can make to their company, and they will question whether you can "hit the ground running." A temporary job, although not as good as a full-time job, still shows the employer you were out there in the market, performing the kind of work that they need at their company.

So – bottom line, I think signing up with temporary agencies is a great option, as long as you don't use them as your only option. If you are working forty hours a week at a company through a temp agency, that makes it more difficult to conduct your job search, but if you are focused on putting in at least a few extra hours each evening and pretty full days on the weekend, then I think they are fine.

> **Don't overlook temp agencies. They may be just what I need.**

I have many friends who own or work at temporary agencies. I asked many of them whether they recommended that job seekers sign up with one or multiple agencies. Every one of them recommended that job seekers sign up with multiple – three or four – temporary agencies. They stressed that each agency has a different set of job requests from the business community, and job seekers would be wise to sign up with several agencies.

Temp Agencies – Yes or No? checklist

_____ There are pros and cons to working through temp agencies.

_____ I should weigh the pros and cons of working for temp agencies.

_____ Generally speaking, temp agencies are good, but they may put a damper on my full-time job search.

_____ If I do decide to work with a temp agency, I should sign up with three or four agencies, not just one.

_____ If I sign up with temp agencies, understand that it is sort of like a test drive and may prove to be an opportunity to earn a full-time job with one of the companies I am temping with.

For High School Grads

The expert in anything was once a beginner.
– Helen Hayes

You haven't yet gone to college? You're just graduating from high school and wonder what you should do? Can't decide whether you should work for a while before going to college? Or should you go to college at all? Would a vocational school be better? How about the military? Or nothing at all? Let's talk about some of those options.

Work for a while before you go to college
This is an option that many young people exercise, some because they just really don't know what to do, and others because financially, college is difficult for them to swing. So they decide to get a job and wait it out for a while.

If you do that, then be careful not to let the money you have in the bank – your savings for college – "burn a hole in your pocket," as my father would say. As you amass a good number of shekels in your bank account, that flashy new car, great apartment, wonderful cruise with friends, etc., may look more and more enticing to you. You must be strong and remember what your higher goal is: to get to college. Also, depending on your family's financial situation, you may be eligible for grants (that is: free money) from the government. Or, there are low-cost student loans available that do not need to be paid back until after you graduate and start work. If the lack of finances is truly what is keeping you from going college, there are a number of options available to you to solve that problem – including what you're doing – saving for college.

Another option is to **attend a local junior college while you are working**. Junior colleges are great places to knock out those general education classes that all universities require at a fraction of the tuition cost those larger universities and colleges charge. And you can often live at home while attending, as well as work part-time.

As you look for work to help you save money and prepare for college, you'll often run into those dratted applications software systems I mention elsewhere in this book. A few years ago, my daughter was looking for a summer job. She shared with me her frustration. She would see a sign in a store that said they were hiring, and she would go in and ask to speak to someone about the position. Typically she was brought to an assistant manager or a manager, who invariably told her she needed to apply online. So she'd come home, apply online and wait. And wait. And no one contacted her. Perhaps you've had a similar experience.

After she told me about what was happening, I suggested that after she applied online, she should then go to the store with her resume (such as it was) and ask to see the manager. She would then introduce herself, explain she had applied online, but that she wanted to stop by and introduce herself so the manager could put a name with the information s/he would receive through the company's application system. Armed with her name / resume / paper application, that manager could seek her application out from the hundreds that were in the system and make a hiring decision. If you try that, I will tell you that the manager / assistant manager will be impressed with how proactive you are. And you can show him / her how excited you are about working with their company. I guarantee you will be one of the few (if any) applicants that does more than applies online and then sits at home and waits for someone to call. This method is a recipe for success!

When I graduated from high school, one of the industries in which young people could make a lot of money quickly was construction. After applying at a number of construction companies and being rejected because of my lack of experience, I hit on a strategy that netted me a job. After introducing myself to the the owner of a small steel construction company, I said something like:

"I do not have much construction experience. However, I have a strong work ethic, have good dexterity (I was a high school athlete), and can learn anything quickly. I will work for half wages until you feel I have gained enough experience for you to pay me full wages."

The owner smiled and said, "Well, how can I beat that! You start on Monday morning." Two weeks later when I received my first paycheck, I was gratified to see that he didn't hold me to my offer to work for half wages – he paid me a full wage.

Should you go to college at all?

Well, that depends…what are your goals in life? If you are looking to have a family, purchase a home, drive a decent car, you may want to strongly consider finishing high school and going to college. Nationally, the statistics indicate the more education you have, the more financially secure you will be.

Recent studies show the following information:

Average Salary at Various Educational Levels

	Average Salary	% working full time	% employment
No HS diploma	$23,000	52%	57%
High School diploma	$33,000	62%	64%
Some college	$37,000	64%	75%
Associate's degree	$40,000	67%	80%
Bachelor's degree	$55,000	72%	88%
Master's degree	$66,000	NA	NA

NA = Not Available

(Information from the National Center for Education Statistics)

The message is clear – a little educational effort now will make a huge difference in your earning capability now and into the future. $10, $14, $15 an hour sounds great right now, while you're living in your parents' basement, or rooming with a buddy, but it's difficult to support a family on as time goes on.

Of course, you would be well advised to check out the average earnings of various career opportunities – attorneys make more than accountants, who make more than architects, who make more than high school teachers, who make more than counselors, who make more than…you get the picture. If you decide college is for you, you may want to research the fields you are most interested in. My advice on a career choice? Don't just chase the money. I have had a job I didn't like before, one that I was ill-matched for, and I was miserable. Don't put yourself in that same situation. Decide what your strengths and interests are, then research the various careers that may be open to you.

What about vocational / trade school?

Through the years, I have learned that college isn't for everyone. If that's the case for you, you may want to look into a vocational / trade school. There are many such schools available in almost any community. The average salary of a trade school grad in 2014 was $43,000. And – placement rates for trade should graduates are close to 100%, while the average placement rate for college grads in this economy is 86%.

The information in the paragraph and table above represents average earnings and employment rates. Your field of education, should you choose to go, may significantly skew from that data. College graduates in education, for example, found their employment rate at 95%, while those who studied architecture had employment rates of about 87%, and graphics artists and history majors were about 90%. Trade schools produce many of the nation's welders, mechanics, graphic artists, massage therapists, construction managers, nurses, aviators, cosmetologists, culinary artists, etc. The wages for these careers are vastly different, so before you jump into any one of the other of these careers, research what the earnings potential for each of them may be and see if that fits your long-term goals.

How about the military?

The military can be a marvelous career if you are interested in serving your country. It can be a life-long career, or it can help you learn and gain skills that you can use outside of the military after you have put in four years. Initial salaries for entry-level ranks in the Army, Air Force, Marines and Navy are not huge – around $1,400 to

$1,700 per month, depending on any experience you may have, education, etc., and the branch of service you are in. Now $1,400 to $1,700 per month doesn't sound like a lot (and it's not!), but you have perks that other jobs don't provide, including military housing (or a housing allowance if you prefer), medical care for yourself and your family, food allowance, and educational benefits.

And – the military option is one way to provide financing for your future educational pursuits. They have several options, including full scholarships (you serve in the military after your education is complete), or monies that are available after you have served.

So if you decide that college or vocational school aren't your cup of tea, you may want to check out the military as an option. There are recruiting offices in most cities that can answer your questions and help you understand what your options and opportunities are.

Those are some of the primary options available to you as you try to figure out what to do as you near the end of your high school career.

For High School Grads checklist

_____ I have several options available to me for next steps after high school. Study them carefully!

_____ If I decide to work to earn money for college, don't be swayed by other options that might present themselves (trips, cars, apartments, etc.)

_____ As I apply for jobs, don't just apply online and sit at home waiting to be contacted – apply online, then go to the place of business and introduce myself.

_____ Generally speaking, the more education I have, the better off I will be financially.

_____ Junior college is a great low-cost way to get my general studies classes done before going to a higher-cost university.

_____ Don't overlook vocational / trade school as a possibility.

_____ Serving in the military is another viable option available to me, and includes an educational benefit if I wish to take advantage of it.

In Summary

Life is very interesting…in the end, some of your greatest pains become your greatest strengths. – Drew Barrymore

We have completed a journey, you and I. Hopefully by following the various suggestions in this book, you have secured employment, or will shortly do so. Before closing this book out, let me just share a few points to remember.

This is a tough economy – you need to be serious about your job hunting responsibilities. As mentioned earlier, your job is to find a job, and you should consider your job as a full-time – 40 hours each week – job. If you don't, before long you'll find you're spending less than 40 hours searching for work…then you'll be spending less than 30 hours searching for work, then less than 20 hours, and before you know it, your job search is just a token effort each week, if that.

You must fight discouragement! Discouragement will lead to an "Oh-what's-the-use" attitude, and you may miss that one marvelous opportunity that is out there for you. As I did, you should adopt the idea that the very next job you apply for will be the one that leads to a great career. Also consider that the job may only be posted today – so be sure and work every day at finding work.

Use your networks! As you hopefully saw earlier in the book, networking is nothing more than reaching out to your acquaintances and letting them know you are seeking for work. Remind them occasionally with weekly e-mails detailing your job search, where you have applied and where you are interviewing. Someone in your network may know someone at the company you have applied to and will put in a good word for you, carry your resume to a hiring manager, etc.

Remember my friend who said his goal was to apply for at least three jobs each day, and how often he found that when he forced himself to apply for that second and third job, how one or both of them yielded an interview.

Be active, be busy, and be positive.

Your resumes need to be tailored for each job you apply to. Don't forget to do a cover letter, and like your resume, it needs to be tailored specifically to the job for which you are applying. One-size-fits-all resumes and cover letters are not effective in this current economic environment.

Differentiate yourself as a candidate. Remember that if a company is considering hiring entry-level employees, they know you will not have much, if any experience. But if you can differentiate yourself – show any volunteer work that is relevant, or things that show your potential employer that you are better than the average candidate – *Employee of the Month*, customer kudos, etc., that may be the edge you need to beat out other candidates who like you, do not have much experience.

And remember, have faith in yourself, your abilities and the value you can add to many companies. As you believe that, it will come through in interviews, cover letters, etc., and hiring managers will believe it as well.

Final Thoughts – Once You're In!

I'd like to end on an upbeat note, with a few words of advice now that you've landed your first job. Live by these simple rules and you hopefully won't have to start looking for a new job any time soon!

First, make a great impression. Arrive early or right on time, and stay all day. Simple, right?

Next, be pleasant and flexible. Establish yourself from the get-go as a hard worker and remember, first impressions are critical, so ... be nice!

Bring important paperwork with you the first day, including your I-9 (a government form every US employer is required to complete for each new employee within three days of their start date) and any other documentation HR tells you in advance they will need. Don't make your new company stalk you for any of this; they will not like it.

Look for opportunities to change the way things are done. You are the "new kid" and can ask "Why?" for a short time. Take advantage of this in a friendly, helpful way.

Finally, keep your nose to the grindstone, head in the game, shoulder to the wheel and all the other bodily metaphors you can think of that mean: *work hard*. You won't regret it!

Good luck and happy hunting!

Index

NOTES

NOTES

NOTES

YOUR FIRST JOB

NOTES

Interested in delving deeper into the topics covered by *Your First Job*? Author Dan
Quillen has put his 25 years of HR hiring experience into *Get a Job! How I Found
a Job When Jobs are Hard to Find – And So Can You*. All aspects of job searching are covered, including resumes, interviews, staying positive, networking, and
much more!

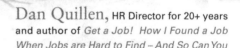